Pocket-guide

to Southern African

MAMMALS

BURGER CILLIÉ

GW00499989

J.L. van Schaik

Dedicated to
my father (Vadie)

Acknowledgements

I would like to thank all the wildlife photographers who generously provided the photographs used in this book. Their names are mentioned on page 124.

Thanks are also due to Kjeld Kruger for allowing me to photograph his collection of dung, as well as to all other people who made available examples of dung.

Special thanks to Kjeld for making the sketches of spoor from examples he collected in the veld.

Burger Cillié

Published by J.L. van Schaik Publishers, 1064 Arcadia Street, Hatfield, Pretoria
All rights reserved
Copyright © 1992 G.E.B. Cillié

First edition 1992
Second impression 1995
Third impression 2000
ISBN 0 624 03833 5

Cover design by Barrett Joubert
Illustrations by Anneliese Burger
Typesetting by ORBiT CC, Pretoria
Reproduction by Al Graphics, Pretoria
Printed and bound by NBD
Drukkery Street, Goodwood 7460, Western Cape

Preface

It is remarkable and satisfying to learn that in South Africa, as in the rest of the world, there is a growing awareness and interest in our oppressed environment and endangered wildlife. As in the past there is a greater interest in mammals than in smaller vertebrate animals, mainly due to their size, large diversity, beauty and interesting habits.

Over the past few years a range of guides by authors, including Smithers, Stuart and Stuart, Pienaar and collaborators, De Graaff, Walker and Burger Cillié, on the identification, lifestyle and habits of a variety of Southern African mammals, have been published. These guides have met the need for more insight into our unique animal kingdom.

One problem, however, with the current series of guides is that they are too large to be carried by fieldworkers and hikers. Burger Cillié has met that need by compiling this complete guide on all the larger and medium sized Southern African mammals. His book is well illustrated and helps the layman to easily identify all the mammals discussed in the text. A short but complete description is given of where the animal can be found, its spoor, dung, differences between the male and female, differences between closely related species, habitat and grazing, habits, details of reproduction, vocalisation and age. It also includes statistics about the animal's weight, shoulder height and record horn lengths (in the case of antelopes and buffalo).

This guide will meet with the approval of hikers, pupils attending veld-schools, prospective fieldrangers and other fieldworkers who constantly need to have a guide at hand.

I therefore recommend this guide to all nature lovers.

Dr U. de V. Pienaar
Former director: National Parks Board

Contents

Introduction

The format of this book has been chosen so that it can fit into your pocket. It has been compiled to serve as a manual for quick identification of not only the animal, but also of any spoor you may come across. To facilitate identification of the animals, reliable sketches of the spoor and photographs of the dung are used.

Only one photograph of each animal is published, except in the cases where the sexes differ, then a photograph of each is published.

All the animals discussed in this guide are found in the geographical area south of the Kunene and Zambesi Rivers.

Also provided is a key to the habitat in which each mammal is found, and this will enable you to trace the animal more quickly in the guide.

Maps of where the animals can be found are also published, and these show the distribution not only of a mammal, but also of its subspecies.

For the trophy hunter, minimum requirements as well as the latest records according to the Rowland Ward (R.W.) and Safari Club International (S.C.I.) systems are given.

This guide will come in handy for the hunter, hiker and nature lover.

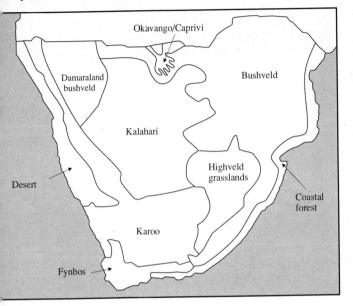

Map labels: Okavango/Caprivi, Damaraland bushveld, Bushveld, Kalahari, Highveld grasslands, Desert, Coastal forest, Karoo, Fynbos

Habitat keys

Only six of the most important vegetation regions are discussed. They are the bushveld (savannah), the Kalahari, the highveld grasslands, the Karoo, the fynbos areas, and the Damaraland bushveld of Namibia. The river/marshes and surrounding floodplains of the Okavango and Caprivi have also been discussed because of the unique occurrence of certain antelope.

Each region has been divided into a number of typical habitat types. The animals that occur in these regions are listed in columns beneath the habitat types.

These keys should be used as an aid towards fast and accurate identification of animals and as an indication of the habitat where a certain animal can be found.

BUSHVELD (savannah)
Antelope

Thicket	Plain	Marsh	River	Koppie
Kudu	Blue wildebeest	Buffalo	Buffalo	Kudu
Nyala	Tsessebe	Licht. hartebeest	Nyala	Eland
Red duiker	Roan antelope	Waterbuck	Waterbuck	Common duiker
Blue duiker	Sable antelope	Reedbuck	Red duiker	Klipspringer
Common duiker	Buffalo	Oribi	Blue duiker	Mntn. reedbuck
Suni	Kudu	Steenbok	Impala	Bushbuck
Licht. hartebeest	Eland	Impala	Common duiker	Sharpe's grysbok

2

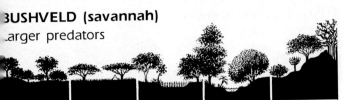

BUSHVELD (savannah)
Larger predators

Thicket	Plain	Marsh	River	Koppie
Side-striped jackal	Cape hunting dog	African civet	Side-striped jackal	Black-backed jackal
African civet	Side-striped jackal	Aardwolf	African civet	Brown hyaena
Spotted hyaena	Black-backed jackal		Spotted hyaena	Leopard
Leopard	Aardwolf		Leopard	Lion
Cheetah	Brown hyaena		Lion	
Lion	Spotted hyaena			

3

BUSHVELD (savannah)
Smaller predators

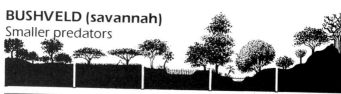

Thicket	Plain	Marsh	River	Koppie
Large-spotted genet	Small-spotted genet	Caracal	Large-spotted genet	Caracal
Serval	Caracal	Yellow mongoose		Striped polecat
African wild cat	African wild cat	Dwarf mongoose	African wild cat	
Striped polecat	Striped polecat	**Marsh and river**		Slender mongoose
Banded mongoose	Yellow mongoose	Small-spotted genet	Serval	
	Slender mongoose	Spotted-necked otter	Cape clawless otter	Honey badger
Honey badger	Dwarf mongoose	Honey badger	White-tailed mongoose	
		Water mongoose	Banded mongoose	

4

BUSHVELD (savannah)
Other larger mammals

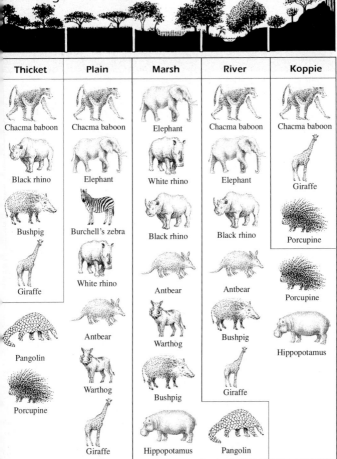

Thicket	Plain	Marsh	River	Koppie
Chacma baboon	Chacma baboon	Elephant	Chacma baboon	Chacma baboon
Black rhino	Elephant	White rhino	Elephant	Giraffe
Bushpig	Burchell's zebra	Black rhino	Black rhino	Porcupine
Giraffe	White rhino	Antbear	Antbear	Porcupine
Pangolin	Antbear	Warthog	Bushpig	Hippopotamus
Porcupine	Warthog	Bushpig	Giraffe	
	Giraffe	Hippopotamus	Pangolin	

5

BUSHVELD (savannah)
Other smaller mammals

Thicket	Plain	Marsh	River	Koppie
S.A. hedgehog	S.A. hedgehog	Springhare	S.A. hedgehog	Vervet monkey
Thick-tailed bushbaby	Lesser bushbaby	Greater cane rat	Thick-tailed bushbaby	Rock dassie
Lesser bushbaby	Cape hare		Lesser bushbaby	Tree squirrel
Vervet monkey	Tree squirrel		Vervet monkey	Scrub hare
Samango monkey	Springhare		Samango monkey	Tree squirrel
Scrub hare	Tree squirrel		Scrub hare	Greater cane rat

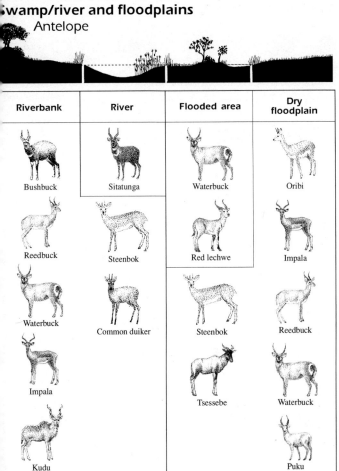

Riverbank	River	Flooded area	Dry floodplain
Bushbuck	Sitatunga	Waterbuck	Oribi
Reedbuck	Steenbok	Red lechwe	Impala
Waterbuck	Common duiker	Steenbok	Reedbuck
Impala		Tsessebe	Waterbuck
Kudu			Puku

HIGHVELD GRASSLAND
Antelope and other smaller mammals

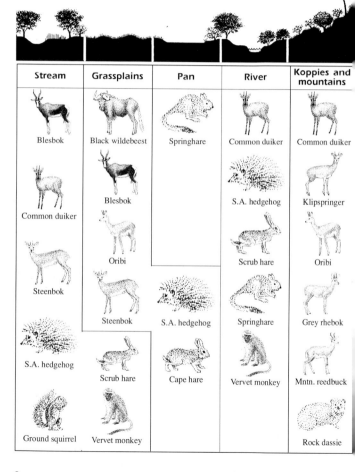

Stream	Grassplains	Pan	River	Koppies and mountains
Blesbok	Black wildebeest	Springhare	Common duiker	Common duiker
Common duiker	Blesbok		S.A. hedgehog	Klipspringer
Steenbok	Oribi		Scrub hare	Oribi
S.A. hedgehog	Steenbok	S.A. hedgehog	Springhare	Grey rhebok
Ground squirrel	Scrub hare	Cape hare	Vervet monkey	Mntn. reedbuck
	Vervet monkey			Rock dassie

Stream	Grassplains	Pan	River	Koppies and mountains
African wild cat	Aardwolf	Aardwolf	African wild cat	Slender mongoose
Striped polecat	Caracal	Caracal	White-tailed mongoose	Brown hyaena
Small-spotted genet	Small spotted cat	Suricate	Water mongoose	Chacma baboon
Slender mongoose	Striped polecat	Yellow mongoose	Chacma baboon	Rock dassie
White-tailed mongoose	Yellow mongoose	Water mongoose	Small-spotted genet	Striped polecat
Water mongoose	Suricate	Black-backed jackal	Cape fox	White rhino
White rhino	Cape fox	White rhino	Black-backed jackal	Antbear

KALAHARI
Antelope

Dry river	Dune land	Plain	Pan
Blue wildebeest	Red hartebeest	Blue wildebeest	Springbok
Common duiker	Springbok	Red hartebeest	Common duiker
Springbok	Steenbok	Springbok	Steenbok
Steenbok	Common duiker	Steenbok	Gemsbok
Gemsbok	Gemsbok	Common duiker	
Kudu	Kudu	Gemsbok	
Eland	Eland		

KALAHARI

Other mammals

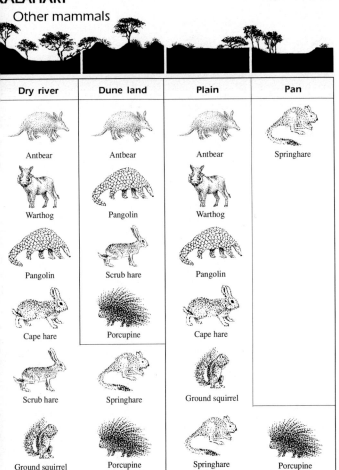

Dry river	Dune land	Plain	Pan
Antbear	Antbear	Antbear	Springhare
Warthog	Pangolin	Warthog	
Pangolin	Scrub hare	Pangolin	
Cape hare	Porcupine	Cape hare	
Scrub hare	Springhare	Ground squirrel	
Ground squirrel	Porcupine	Springhare	Porcupine

11

KALAHARI
Predators

Dry river	Dune land	Plain	Pan
Bat-eared fox	Honey badger	Bat-eared fox	Cape fox
Cape hunting dog	Bat-eared fox	Black-backed jackal	Aardwolf
Black-backed jackal	Cape hunting dog	Aardwolf	Suricate
Small-spotted genet	Cape fox	Spotted hyaena	Yellow mongoose
Aardwolf	Black-backed jackal	Cheetah	Caracal
Brown hyaena	Small-spotted genet	Yellow mongoose	Small-spotted genet

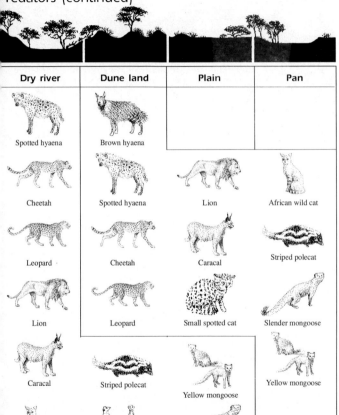

Dry river	Dune land	Plain	Pan
Spotted hyaena	Brown hyaena		
Cheetah	Spotted hyaena	Lion	African wild cat
Leopard	Cheetah	Caracal	Striped polecat
Lion	Leopard	Small spotted cat	Slender mongoose
Caracal	Striped polecat	Yellow mongoose	Yellow mongoose
African wild cat	Suricate	Slender mongoose	

13

DAMARALAND BUSHVELD
Antelope

Pan and floodplain	Woodland	Thickets	Stream/river	Koppie
Blue wildebeest	Blue wildebeest	Common duiker	Common duiker	Common duiker
Red hartebeest	Red hartebeest	Damara dik-dik	Black-faced inpala	Klipspringer
Springbok	Springbok	Black-faced impala	Kudu	Damara dik-dik
Steenbok	Steenbok	Kudu	Eland	Kudu
Gemsbok	Black-faced impala			Eland
	Gemsbok	Kudu		

14

Pan and floodplain	Woodland	Thickets	Stream/river	Koppie
Burchell's zebra	Elephant	Chacma baboon	Elephant	Chacma baboon
Antbear	Burchell's zebra	Elephant	White rhino	Mountain zebra
Warthog	White rhino	Black rhino	Black rhino	Porcupine
Pangolin	Antbear	Giraffe	Antbear	Scrub hare
Ground squirrel	Warthog	S.A. hedgehog	Warthog	Vervet monkey
Springhare	Giraffe	Vervet monkey	Scrub hare	Scrub hare
Porcupine	Pangolin	Springhare		

15

DAMARALAND BUSHVELD

Predators

Pan and floodplain	Woodland	Thickets	Stream/river	Koppie
Bat-eared fox	Small-spotted genet	Brown hyaena	Brown hyaena	Honey badger
Cape fox	Leopard	Leopard	Spotted hyaena	Striped polecat
Aardwolf	African wild cat	African wild cat	Lion	Caracal
Suricate	Slender mongoose	Striped polecat	African wild cat	Slender mongoose
Yellow mongoose	Banded mongoose	Slender mongoose	Banded mongoose	Banded mongoose

Pan, floodplain and woodland

Black-backed jackal	Brown hyaena	Spotted hyaena
Cheetah	Lion	Caracal

Stream/river and koppie

Black-backed jackal	Small-spotted genet
Honey badger	Leopard

16

Coastal plain	River	Plateau	Mountain slope
Bat-eared fox	Black-backed jackal	Bat-eared fox	Large-spotted genet
Cape fox	Large-spotted genet	Cape fox	Leopard
Black-backed jackal	Leopard	Black-backed jackal	African wild cat
Small-spotted genet	Small-spotted genet	Small-spotted genet	Striped polecat
Aardwolf	African wildcat	Aardwolf	Honey badger
Caracal	Striped polecat	Cape clawless otter	Caracal	Striped polecat
Honey badger	Yellow mongoose	Honey badger	Water mongoose	Yellow mongoose

FYNBOS
Antelope and other mammals

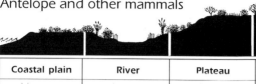

Coastal plain	River	Plateau	Mountain slope
Bontebok	Common duiker	Bontebok	Common duiker
Springbok	Cape grysbok	Springbok	Klipspringer
Steenbok	Scrub hare	Steenbok	Cape grysbok
Cape grysbok	Grey rhebok	Rock dassie	Grey rhebok
Grey rhebok	Mountain zebra	Cape hare	Chacma baboon
Rock dassie	Cape hare	Scrub hare	Mountain zebra
Antbear	Porcupine	Porcupine	Porcupine	Rock dassie

18

Antelope and other mammals

Mountain slope	Plain	Pan	Koppie	Stream/river
Common duiker	Springbok	Springbok	Klipspringer	Common duiker
Klipspringer	Steenbok	Gemsbok	Kudu	Steenbok
Grey rhebok	Gemsbok	Cape hare	Mntn. reedbuck	Kudu
Kudu	Ground squirrel	Antbear	Mountain zebra	Chacma baboon
Mntn. reedbuck	Cape hare	Scrub hare	Rock dassie	Vervet monkey
Chacma baboon	Rock dassie	Porcupine	Antbear	Black rhino
Mountain zebra	Scrub hare	Porcupine	Scrub hare	Ground squirrel

19

KARROO
Predators

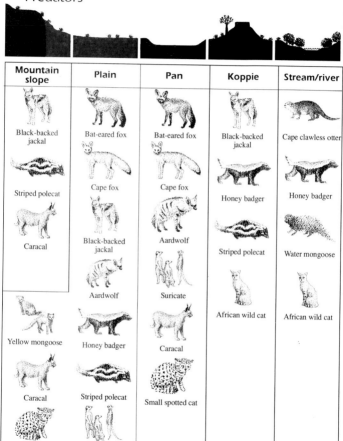

Mountain slope	Plain	Pan	Koppie	Stream/river
Black-backed jackal	Bat-eared fox	Bat-eared fox	Black-backed jackal	Cape clawless otter
Striped polecat	Cape fox	Cape fox	Honey badger	Honey badger
Caracal	Black-backed jackal	Aardwolf	Striped polecat	Water mongoose
Yellow mongoose	Aardwolf	Suricate	African wild cat	African wild cat
Caracal	Honey badger	Caracal		
Small spotted cat	Striped polecat	Small spotted cat		
	Suricate			

20

OUTH AFRICAN HEDGEHOG *Atelerix frontalis*

A. KRIMPVARKIE)

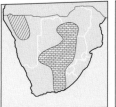

SUBSPECIES

▨ *A.f. frontalis*

▧ *A.f. angolae*

Mass: 236–480 g

Length: ± 20 cm

IDENTIFICATION: The upper parts of the body are covered with black and white dull yellow ringed spines. The white framed face ends in a pointed snout.

DIFFERENCE BETWEEN ♂ AND ♀: None.

HABITAT: Dry shelter for nests, enough insects and other food are essential. Occurs a variety of habitats in bush savannah and grassland. Avoids moist soil. Independent of water.

HABITS: Mainly nocturnal, but appears during the day, especially after rain, to feed on earthworms (which move to the surface) and insects. Becomes torpid during winter. Rests during the day in piles of debris or in holes, changing resting places daily. The only semipermanent nests are those used by the female to nurse a litter, and during winter when hibernating. Poor eyesight but keen sense of smell to locate food just below the surface.

FOOD: Mainly millipedes, centipedes, beetles, termites, moths, locusts and earth-worms. Sometimes also chicks of small ground-living birds, small mice, lizards, bird's eggs, snails, frogs and fungi. Drinks water when available.

VOCALISATION: High-pitched alarm; snorts, sniffs and growls when they meet.

BREEDING: 1–9 young are born from October–April after a gestation period of ± 5 weeks. ♀ has 2 pairs of breast and 1 pair of abdominal mammae.

AGE: ± 3 years.

21

THICK-TAILED BUSHBABY *Otolemur crassicaudatus*

(BOSNAGAAP)

SUBSPECIES

▨ *O.c. crassicaudatus:*
Slightly reddish-brown on back

▨ *O.c. monteiri:*
Upper parts yellowish, under parts ash-grey

Mass: ♂ ± 1,22 kg
♀ ± 1,13 kg
Length: ♂ ± 74 cm
♀ ± 73 cm

IDENTIFICATION: The largest of the two bushbabies. Huge eyes and broad rounded mobile ears. The fur is long and soft, especially at the tail.

DIFFERS FROM OTHER SPECIES: Lesser bushbaby: Smaller, fur less fluffy and tail not so thick. Utilizes different habitat types.

DIFFERENCE BETWEEN ♂ AND ♀: The male is slightly larger than the female.

HABITAT: Mountain forest, forest and dense woodland in areas with a high rainfall. Found even in riverine forests surrounded by arid country, e.g. in the Transvaal.

HABITS: Nocturnal: appears after sunset and is periodically active at night. First grooms itself after appearing. Gregarious – usually found in family groups that rest high up in thick foliage during the day. Forages alone. Urinates on its feet and hands and also rubs mammary glands against branches or other bushbabies as a means of scent-marking its home range.

FOOD: Fruit such as wild figs, mobola plums and kudu-berries. Also gum, insects and occasionally birds and reptiles.

VOCALISATION: Repeated ominous hoarse wailing which is heard over a considerable distance, slightly resembles a child's crying. Alarm call: a shrill scream.

BREEDING: Normally 2 young are born during August–September (Tvl: November) after a gestation period of ± 4 months. ♀ has 1 pair of breast and 1 pair of groin mammae.

AGE: Unknown.

LESSER BUSHBABY *Galago moholi*
(NAGAPIE)

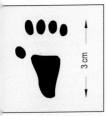

Mass:	♂ ± 155 g
	♀ ± 150 g
Length:	♂ ± 37 cm
	♀ ± 36 cm

IDENTIFICATION: The smallest of the two bushbabies. Huge eyes; the large ears are membranaceous and very mobile. It has a long tail and fluffy fur.

DIFFERS FROM OTHER SPECIES: Thick-tailed bushbaby: Larger, with longer, softer fur, especially on the tail. Utilizes different habitat.

DIFFERENCE BETWEEN ♂ AND ♀: The male is slightly larger than the female.

HABITAT: A savannah species: prefers mopani and especially acacia savannah along rivers and tributaries. Thorn trees shelter numerous insects and supply gum, both of which are essential for its diet. Old thorn and mopani tree trunks have holes and hollows which serve as shelter for bushbabies. Independent of water.

HABITS: Mainly nocturnal: active during the first and last parts of the night. Small groups rest during the day in nests or holes in trees; at night individuals forage on their own. Active during the first and last parts of the night. Dominant animals in particular urinate on their hands and feet and also rub their mammary glands against other bushbabies. It can take immense leaps while moving from tree to tree.

FOOD: Gum is essential. Also insects such as locusts, moths, beetles and spiders. Does not take in water – gets enough liquid in diet.

VOCALISATION: Growl, low-pitched alarm call and "chak-chak" noises.

BREEDING: 1–2 (sometimes 3) young are born in Oct./Nov. and/or Jan./Feb. after a gestation period of just over 4 months.   **AGE:** ± 10 years.

CHACMA BABOON *Papio ursinus*

(KAAPSE BOBBEJAAN)

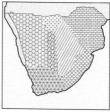

Mass: ♂ 27–44 kg
      ♀ 14–17 kg
Shoulder ♂ ± 71 cm
height: ♀ ± 61 cm

IDENTIFICATION: Long legs and an elongated face with the eyes close to one another. Has pink callosites and a sickle tail.

DIFFERENCE BETWEEN ♂ AND ♀: The male is larger and more aggressive than the female.

HABITAT: Prefers cliffs or tall trees for shelter and also sufficient water for drinking. Consequently prefers mountains, hills, riverine forests and various types of savannah with enough food.

HABITS: Troops vary from about 20 animals with one dominant male to 100 with 12 dominant males. These adult males are prominent in most of the activities, e.g troop movement, chasing and fighting, mating, grooming, guarding and maintaining a strict hierarchy. They forage during the day, leaving their sleeping sites just after sunrise and returning in the late afternoon.

FOOD: Grass, leaves, bulbs, roots, gum, wild fruit, mushrooms, berries, scorpions, snails, insects and meat. Drinks water regularly.

VOCALISATION: Males have a bisyllabic bark; the others chatter and shriek.

BREEDING: 1 (seldom 2) young are born throughout the year after a gestation period of ± 6 months. ♀ has 1 pair of breast mammae.

AGE: ± 18 years.

VERVET MONKEY *Cercopithecus aethiops*

(BLOUAAP)

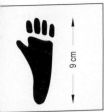

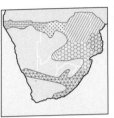

IDENTIFICATION: Small black face, a conspicuous long tail ending in a dark brown tip and the male's scrotum is blue.

DIFFERS FROM OTHER SPECIES: Samango monkey: Larger and browner with black legs and shoulders.

DIFFERENCE BETWEEN ♂ AND ♀: The male is larger than the female.

HABITAT: A savannah species: prefers fairly dense savannah – the ecotone between savannah and forest and riverine forest, even if surrounded by unfavourable terrain. Water, sufficient fruit-bearing trees and trees for shelter are requirements.

HABITS: Troops consist of up to 20 animals with an apparent hierarchy. The higher in social ranking the more readily they are recognised. They have a strong sense of coherence, which is reinforced by mutual grooming. They sleep in tall trees and forage early in the mornings and again later in the afternoons, returning to their sleeping sites well before sunset.

FOOD: Wild fruit: Jackal-berry, wild figs, marula and sour-plum. Pods of camel thorn and mopani, as well as gum, birds, eggs and insects.

VOCALISATION: Chatters or stutters as an alarm call. Young also squeal.

BREEDING: 1 (rarely 2) young are born at any time of the year after a gestation period of ± 7 months. ♀ has 1 pair of breast mammae.

AGE: ± 12 years.

25

SAMANGO MONKEY *Cercopithecus mitis*

(SAMANGO-AAP)

Mass:	♂	8,2–10 kg
	♀	4,5–5,2 kg
Shoulder	♂	± 39 cm
height:	♀	± 35 cm

IDENTIFICATION: Legs, shoulders and end part of the tail are black. Hind leg are very long, and the body slants forward when all four feet are on the ground.

DIFFERS FROM OTHER SPECIES: Vervet monkey: Smaller, more greyish with a black face. Male's scrotum is blue.

DIFFERENCE BETWEEN ♂ AND ♀: The male is larger than the female.

HABITAT: Prefers dense coastal forest, mountain forest and riverine forest (even dry forest) – leaves this habitat only in search of food or when moving to another habitat. Dense forests with tall trees for shelter and trees which provide food are essential.

HABITS: Troops vary between 4 (with 1 adult male) and 34 (with 3 or more adult males). Sleep in tall trees at night and intermittently forage during the day. Bask in the morning sun before going out to forage. Usually rest during the heat of the day. The males guard the troop when it moves out. Mutual aggression seldom occurs.

FOOD: Gum of thorn trees, leaves, berries, shoots, soft seed-pods, wild fruit, caterpillars and other insects.

VOCALISATION: "Boom" and repeated "nyah" sounds are heard the most.

BREEDING: A single young is born from September–April after a gestation period of ± 4 months. ♀ has 1 pair of breast mammae.

AGE: Unknown.

AT-EARED FOX   *Otocyon megalotis*
(AKOORVOS)

Mass:	♂ 3,4–4,9 kg
	♀ 3,2–5,3 kg
Shoulder	
height:	± 30 cm

DENTIFICATION: Very large rounded ears, bushy tail with black tip, a fluffy oat; the lower parts of the legs are black.

DIFFERS FROM OTHER SPECIES: Cape fox: Of lighter build, lighter in colour light brown), especially the legs, and has a silvery sheen. The ears are smaller.

DIFFERENCE BETWEEN ♂ AND ♀: The female is slightly heavier than the male.

HABITAT: Found in arid areas, open grassplains, open woodland with short grass and bare patches, as well as scattered shrubveld in the Karoo. The presence of har-vester termites is essential. Independent of water.

HABITS: Occur in pairs or small family groups up to 6. Are nocturnal and diurnal, usually resting during the heat of day in holes, patches of tall grass or beneath shrubs. Keen hearing: it digs up underground larvae by listening to their movements. Owing to its skill in twisting and turning at high speed it was given the Afrikaans name of "draaijakkals" (turning jackal).

FOOD: Mainly insects such as harvester termites, locusts and larvae. Also scorpions, mice, reptiles, wild fruit, spiders and millipedes.

VOCALISATION: "Who-who" crying sound. A sharp knocking sound by young ones in distress.

BREEDING: 2–6 young are born from September–November after a gestation period of ± 2 months. ♀ has 2 pairs of groin mammae.   **AGE:** ± 12 years.

27

WILD DOG (Cape hunting dog) *Lycaon pictus*
(WILDEHOND)

8,5 cm

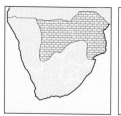

SUBSPECIES
None.

Mass: 20–32 kg

**Shoulder
height:** ± 68 cm

IDENTIFICATION: Dog-like animals with large rounded ears. The coats have white, yellow, brown and black blotches. The end half of the tail is white.
DIFFERS FROM OTHER SPECIES: Spotted hyaena: Larger with black/brown spots, no white. Sloping back; the tail is shorter and dark brown and the ears are smaller.
DIFFERENCE BETWEEN ♂ AND ♀: None.
HABITAT: Prefers grassplains or open woodland and avoids thickets and tall grass. Requires open areas and availability of its principal food is essential. Relatively scarce in areas containing large numbers of lions and spotted hyaenas. Independent of water.
HABITS: Gregarious – hunts in packs, chases prey and tears it apart while still running. Also feeds the rest of the pack by regurgitating some of the meat when returning to the den. Lives in packs of 10–15; packs of up to 40 have been recorded. Diurnal, hunts in early morning or afternoons.
FOOD: Anything from scrub hare and lambs to kudu and blue wildebeest, especially impala and springbok. Drinks water when available.
VOCALISATION: Excited chattering and well-known "who-who" sound.
BREEDING: 7–10 (even 19) puppies are born from March–July after a gestation period of ± 2 months. ♀ has 6 or 7 pairs of mammae.
AGE: ± 10 years.

CAPE FOX *Vulpes chama*
(ILWERVOS)

5 cm

Mass: ♂ ± 2,8 kg
♀ ± 2,5 kg
**Shoulder
height:** ± 33 cm

IDENTIFICATION: Small build, light brown to silverish grey, large ears and a broad bushy tail with a black tip.

DIFFERS FROM OTHER SPECIES: Bat-eared fox: Larger, darker in colour, with black limbs and large ears. Black-backed jackal: Larger, red-brown with dark saddle.

DIFFERENCE BETWEEN ♂ AND ♀: The male is slightly heavier than the female.

HABITAT: Open grassveld with patches of shrubs and open dry thornveld or Karroo shrubveld. Less frequent in open bushveld and Cape fynbos. Frequents grassveld round dry pans in Botswana. Independent of water.

HABITS: Solitary, quite asocial and never groom one another. Mainly nocturnal; active periods are just before sunrise and just after sunset. Rests in holes or tall grass during daytime. Digs its own shelter or adapts an old springhare hole. As home areas overlap it defends only a small territory around the hole in which the young are raised.

FOOD: Smaller mammals (especially mice). Also insects, spiders, reptiles and birds.

VOCALISATION: A bark and a high-pitched crying sound.

BREEDING: 1–5 young are born from October–November after a gestation period of ± 2 months. ♀ has 1 pair of groin and 2 pairs of abdominal mammae.

AGE: Unknown.

SIDE-STRIPED JACKAL *Canis adustus*

(WITKWASJAKKALS)

Mass: ♂ 7,3–12 kg
♀ 7,3–10 kg
Shoulder height: ± 39 cm

IDENTIFICATION: A white stripe on the flanks (sometimes also a dark strip below) which leads to its name "side-striped". The bushy tail ends in a white tip.

DIFFERS FROM OTHER SPECIES: Black-backed jackal: Reddish on the flank and legs; has dark "saddle" on the back.

DIFFERENCE BETWEEN ♂ AND ♀: The male is slightly heavier than the female

HABITAT: Usually in well-watered areas. Generally prefers woodland, thickets valleys and thickly wooded areas. Avoids open grassplains, forests and mountainou areas. Dependent on water.

HABITS: More nocturnal than black-backed jackal, active during greatest part c the night and sometimes seen just before sunset and after sunrise. Solitary, althoug pairs or mother with young are sometimes seen. Rest during the day under a cair or in old antbear holes.

FOOD: Carrion, wild fruit (such as wild figs), scrub hare, mice, moles, insects, bird and lizards.

VOCALISATION: A series of short "nyah-nyah" sounds, the first "nyah" not s drawn out as that of the black-backed jackal.

BREEDING: 2–6 young are born from August–January after a gestation period o 2–2½ months. ♀ has 2 pairs of groin mammae.

AGE: ± 11 years.

BLACK-BACKED JACKAL *Canis mesomelas*
(ROOIJAKKALS)

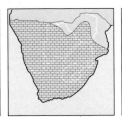

SUBSPECIES

Only one subspecies occurs in this region.

▨ *C.m. mesomelas*

Mass: ♂ 6,8–11,4 kg
♀ 5,5–10 kg

Shoulder height: ± 38 cm

IDENTIFICATION: Light reddish brown (cf. Afrikaans name "rooijakkals"). The "saddle" on its back is black with white speckles.

DIFFERS FROM OTHER SPECIES: Side-striped jackal: A white stripe (sometimes also a dark stripe below) on the flanks; the tail ends in a white tip.

DIFFERENCE BETWEEN ♂ AND ♀: The male is slightly heavier than the female.

HABITAT: Utilizes a variety of habitat types that provide sufficient food. Prefers open arid areas such as woodland, or grassland with enough shrubs. In Botswana it avoids the well-watered areas in the north (Okavango). Independent of water.

HABITS: Diurnal and nocturnal. Mainly seen at sunset and sunrise. Although they are usually solitary, they live in pairs and establish a territory. Both the male and female defend and mark this area. They are scavengers and gather around a carcass. Rest during the day in old antbear holes, between rocks or in cliffs. Shy and cunning with a keen sense of smell.

FOOD: Carrion, lambs, mice, hares, springhare, locusts, crickets, beetles, termites and wild fruit. Can stay without water but drinks it when available.

VOCALISATION: A drawn out "nyah-nyah" sound, interspersed with short "nya-nya" sounds.

BREEDING: 1–6 (rarely 9) young are born from July–October after a gestation period of ± 2 months. ♀ has 2 pairs of groin mammae.   **AGE:** ± 13 years.

CAPE CLAWLESS OTTER *Aonyx capensis*

(GROOTOTTER)

SUBSPECIES

Only one subspecies
occurs in the region.

 A.c. capensis

Mass: 10–18 kg

Length: ± 130 cm

IDENTIFICATION: Aquatic. A long broad tail and a large broad head. The throat and the sides of the face under the eyes and ears are white.

DIFFERS FROM OTHER SPECIES: Spotted-necked otter: Has claws on all four feet; white spots on the throat and lacks the white on the throat and sides of face.

DIFFERENCE BETWEEN ♂ AND ♀: None.

HABITAT: Rivers, lakes, swamps, dams, small streams and even the sea. Aquatic areas with enough food and an environment offering adequate shelter to rest in is essential. Wanders further from water than spotted-necked otter.

HABITS: Usually solitary – diurnal and nocturnal – especially at twilight. Rests in dry shelter or among reeds when it is warm. Spends a great part of its life in water. Usually swims on the surface but can also dive for long periods. After swimming it will lie down in the sun to dry.

FOOD: Mainly frogs and crabs, also fish, octopuses, insects, birds and reptiles. Fish are eaten headfirst, while spotted-necked otter starts at the tail.

VOCALISATION: A high-pitched scream, aggressive hiss and growl and a contented "purring" sound.

BREEDING: 1 (sometimes 2) young are born throughout the year after a gestation period of ± 9 weeks. ♀ has 2 pairs of breast mammae.

AGE: ± 15 years.

SPOTTED-NECKED OTTER *Lutra maculicollis*
(KLEINOTTER)

SUBSPECIES

▦ *L.m. maculicollis:*
Body: chestnut
brown

▨ *L.m. chobiensis:*
More reddish-brown

Mass:	♂	± 4,5 kg
	♀	± 3,5 kg
Length:		± 100 cm

IDENTIFICATION: Aquatic. Elongated, slim build and a broad head. The lower part of the body is brown with white spots on the chest and throat, hence its name.

DIFFERS FROM OTHER SPECIES: Cape clawless otter: No claws on the front feet. The throat and sides of the face under the eyes and ears are white.

DIFFERENCE BETWEEN ♂ AND ♀: The male is larger than the female.

HABITAT: Large perennial rivers, lakes and swamps with large stretches of open water. Never wanders far from water (as shelters and latrines are close to water). Not found in sea water and estuaries.

HABITS: More closely confined to water than the Cape clawless otter. Clumsy on land; only leaves the water to rest, breed or to excrete. Very swift in the water; elegant swimmers. Sometimes hides food on land to eat later. Usually solitary, sometimes found in family groups. Generally active at twilight and with some activity during day and night. Rests and breeds in holes or deep crevasses.

FOOD: Mainly fish. Also crabs, molluscs, frogs and birds. Fish are usually eaten starting at the tail (the clawless otter starts at the head).

VOCALISATION: High squeaking sound ending in vibration and excited whistle.

BREEDING: Usually 2 (seldom 3) young are born from November–December. ♀ has 2 pairs of abdominal mammae.

AGE: Unknown.

HONEY BADGER (Ratel) *Mellivora capensis*

(RATEL)

Mass: 7,9–14,5 kg

**Shoulder
height:** ± 26,5 cm

IDENTIFICATION: Stocky build with short legs. Upper parts of the body are whitish-grey to light brown and the rest of the body is black. Skin is loose, thick and very tough.

DIFFERENCE BETWEEN ♂ AND ♀: None.

HABITAT: Occurs in a variety of habitat types; even very arid parts. Prefers open areas on rocky hills, in shrubby sandveld, grassland, open woodland, scattered riverine forests and floodplains – e.g. around the Okavango swamps. Avoids mountain forests and deserts. Independent of water.

HABITS: Mainly nocturnal, but is often seen during the day. Generally solitary but also seen in pairs. Very brave and will even attack animals larger than themselves. Rests during the day and hunts at night. Moves with a rolling gait, with its snout held close to the ground. The small honey-guide sometimes leads it to a bees' nest.

FOOD: Very fond of honey and bee larvae. Also meat, scorpions, fruit, birds, insects, reptiles, mice and spiders.

VOCALISATION: A high-pitched bark; growls, grunts and makes a nasal "harr-harr" sound.

BREEDING: Usually 2 young are born between October and January after a gestation period of ± 6 months. ♀ has 2 pairs of groin mammae.

AGE: ± 24 years.

STRIPED POLECAT *Ictonyx striatus*
(STINK MUISHOND)

Mass: ♂ 681–1460 g
♀ 596–880 g
Shoulder height: ± 10 cm

IDENTIFICATION: Parallel black and white bands along its back. The body and the tail have long hair. White patches below the ears.

DIFFERS FROM OTHER SPECIES: Striped weasel: Smaller with shorter hair, sinuous body and lacks the white patches below the ears.

DIFFERENCE BETWEEN ♂ AND ♀: The male is larger than the female.

HABITAT: Adaptable: utilizes many habitat types, but never abundantly. Found along dry streams running through deserts, in shrubveld to open grassland, open woodland, thorn thickets, on rocky hills, in forests. Independent of water.

HABITS: Usually solitary, seldom in pairs. Nocturnal, appears only well into the night. Moves sinuously. Digs its own shelter in soft soil but usually takes shelter in old springhare holes, rock piles or fallen tree logs. When disturbed, stands on its hind-legs to observe the area. Uses the well-known, unpleasant, nauseating exudation as its last resort in defence.

FOOD: Mainly mice and insects. Also birds, frogs, reptiles, scorpions, spiders and millipedes.

VOCALISATION: Growls and barks.

BREEDING: 1–3 young are born from October–March after a gestation period of 5–6 weeks. ♀ has 1 pair of abdominal and 1 pair of groin mammae.

AGE: ± 8 years.

AFRICAN CIVET *Civettictis civetta*
(AFRIKAANSE SIWET)

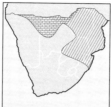

SUBSPECIES

C.c. australis

C.c. volkmanni

Mass: ♂ 9,5–13,2 kg
♀ 9,7–20 kg
Shoulder height: ± 40 cm

IDENTIFICATION: Cat-like animal. Whitish-grey body with black spots merging to stripes on the hindquarters. Black around the eyes with white spots on either side of the nose.

DIFFERENCE BETWEEN ♂ AND ♀: The female is slightly heavier than the male.

HABITAT: Prefers areas with sufficient undergrowth, trees and shrubs bearing fruit and that lure insects. Requires enough shelter such as tall grass, wooded areas, thickets (especially with palms) and reeds. Found more frequently in places where there is permanent water.

HABITS: Exclusively nocturnal and very shy. Active for a period after sunset and also at sunrise. Not a very keen tree climber – depends on fruit falling down naturally or as the result of the actions of other animals or birds. Mainly solitary; uses footpaths that are also used by other civets and deposits its excreta in latrines next to the paths. Stands quite still or lies down flat when disturbed. Smells and hears very well.

FOOD: Insects, wild fruit, mice, reptiles, birds and frogs.

VOCALISATION: Usually silent. A loud coughing bark, a low threatening growl, a scream when fighting and a low "woof" sound.

BREEDING: 1–4 young are born from August–December after a gestation period of ± 2 months. ♀ has 2 pairs of abdominal mammae.

AGE: ± 12 years.

SMALL-SPOTTED GENET *Genetta genetta*

(KLEINKOLMUSKEJAATKAT)

2,5–3 cm

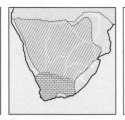

SUBSPECIES

▦ *G.g. felina:* Black spots

▨ *G.g. pulchra:* More reddish-brown spots

Mass: ± 1,9 kg

Shoulder height: ± 15 cm

IDENTIFICATION: A very small cat-like animal, with a long body and short legs. The long tail has black rings ending in a white tip.

DIFFERS FROM OTHER SPECIES: Large-spotted genet: Larger spots on the body, a white chin and the tail ends in a black tip.

DIFFERENCE BETWEEN ♂ AND ♀: None.

HABITAT: Occurs in open arid areas, where large-spotted genet are absent. Prefers woodlands with open grasslands or dry marshes, riverine forests and dry shrubby woodland. Needs enough shelter in the environment such as shrubs, undergrowth and holes in the ground or in trees for resting in. Independent of water.

HABITS: Exclusively nocturnal and mainly solitary, but also seen in pairs. It is terrestrial but is also a keen tree climber when hunting or seeking shelter. Rests in holes in the ground during the day (when trees are not available). Runs fast with its head down and tail held horizontally.

FOOD: Insects such as beetles and locusts, mice and rats, spiders, snakes and birds. Sometimes frogs, fruit and centipedes.

VOCALISATION: Growls and spits.

BREEDING: 2–4 young are born from August–April after a gestation period of 10–11 weeks. ♀ has 2 pairs of abdominal mammae.

AGE: ± 12 years.

37

LARGE-SPOTTED GENET (Rusty-spotted genet) *Genetta tigrina*
(ROOIKOLMUSKEJAATKAT)

SUBSPECIES

▓ *G.t. tigrina:* Large spots, hind feet black

▨ *G.t. rubiginosa:* Usually more rusty-brown spots

▧ *G.t. zambesiana:* Hind feet not black

Mass: 1,4–3,2 kg

Shoulder height: ± 15 cm

IDENTIFICATION: A very small cat-like animal with a long body, short legs and a long black banded tail ending in a black tip.

DIFFERS FROM OTHER SPECIES: Small-spotted genet: Crest of long dark hair on the back, chin is dark and the tail ends in a white tip.

DIFFERENCE BETWEEN ♂ AND ♀: None.

HABITAT: Prefers riverine forests and woodlands, usually avoiding open plains and dry marshes in contrast to the small-spotted genet. Occurs more generally in well watered areas with a high rainfall (450+ mm/annum). Dependent on water.

HABITS: Exclusively nocturnal and appears only long after sunset. Rests during the day in holes in trees, tree trunks or in old antbear or springhare holes. Mainly solitary and usually walks slowly and stealthily. When disturbed or hunting it takes to the trees and leaps for distances of up to 4 metres from tree to tree. It sometimes stands on its hindlegs to observe the surroundings.

FOOD: Mice, locusts, beetles, crickets, spiders, scorpions, frogs, centipedes and wild fruit.

VOCALISATION: Growls and spits.

BREEDING: 2–5 young are born from August–March after a gestation period of ± 2 months. ♀ has 2 pairs of abdominal mammae.

AGE: ± 13 years.

38

SURICATE *Suricata suricatta*
(STOKSTERTMEERKAT)

SUBSPECIES

▦ *S.s. suricatta:* Darker, dark brown around the eyes

▨ *S.s. marjoriae:* Paler, stripes on back lighter, white around eyes

Mass: 620–960 g

Length: ± 50 cm

IDENTIFICATION: Round head with short pointed nose and distinctive slender tapering dark-tipped tail. Dark rings around the eyes and dull dark bands on the lower back.

DIFFERS FROM OTHER SPECIES: Ground squirrel: Distinctive white stripes on the flanks and the bushy tail has long hair.

DIFFERENCE BETWEEN ♂ AND ♀: None.

HABITAT: Open arid areas. Prefers hard or calcareous soil to dig its burrows. In northern Cape it frequents the banks of dry pans. Avoids mountainous areas. Independent of water.

HABITS: Diurnal, only appearing from its hole once the sun has reached it, after which it first sunbathes for a while. Playful and lives in colonies of up to 20 animals, usually occupying a burrow dug by ground squirrels, or sometimes sharing it with ground squirrels or yellow mongooses.

FOOD: Worms, insect larvae, small snakes, snake eggs, lizards, spiders, scorpions, centipedes and millipedes.

VOCALISATION: Loud bark as alarm call, constant grunting while foraging.

BREEDING: 2–5 young are born form October–March after a gestation period of 10–11 weeks. ♀ has 3 pairs of abdominal mammae.

AGE: ± 12 years.

YELLOW MONGOOSE *Cynictis penicillata*

(WITKWASMUISHOND)

Mass: 440–900 g

Length: ± 55 cm

IDENTIFICATION: Colour varies from yellow- or reddish-brown, with a white tipped tail to greyish without the white tail tip.

DIFFERS FROM OTHER SPECIES: Selous mongoose: Smaller, nocturnal and the last three-quarters of the tail is white. Slender mongoose: Tail is less bushy and ends in a black tip.

DIFFERENCE BETWEEN ♂ AND ♀: None.

HABITAT: Open plains in the Karroo, grassplains of the Free State, semidesert shrubby veld in Botswana and grassplains in Namibia. In woodland it prefers open grass patches such as those around water holes. Independent of water.

HABITS: Mainly diurnal and forms colonies of 20 or more animals. Often shares the burrows with ground squirrels and/or suricates, but can dig its own burrow. Forages further away from its burrow than the other two species and makes use of temporary shelter in case of emergency.

FOOD: Beetles, beetle larvae, termites, mice, insects, crickets, caterpillars, ants, locusts, birds, reptiles and ground-living birds.

VOCALISATION: Unknown.

BREEDING: 2–5 young are born from October–March after a gestation period of ± 8 weeks. ♀ has 3 pairs of abdominal mammae.

AGE: ± 12 years.

SLENDER MONGOOSE *Galerella sanguinea*

(WARTKWASMUISHOND)

IDENTIFICATION: Solitary. Colour varies from reddish-brown to dark brown and grey. The tail is very long, thin and has a black tip turning upwards.

DIFFERS FROM OTHER SPECIES: Yellow mongoose: Gregarious; its tail is more bushy and usually ends in a white tip. Meller's mongoose: Tail is much shorter and the hair is much longer. Sometimes has a black tail.

DIFFERENCE BETWEEN ♂ AND ♀: The male is larger than the female.

HABITAT: Not choosy in its habitat requirements. Usually found in open areas to woodlands and even up to the edge of forests. Prefers areas with sufficient shelter such as anthills, rocks or holes in hollow tree trunks.

HABITS: Mainly diurnal, becoming active when it is warmer. Although terrestrial it can climb trees when hunting or frightened. Usually moves quickly, using footpaths. Freezes or stands up on its hindlegs when disturbed in order to investigate.

FOOD: Locusts, termites, beetles, ants, lizards, mice and wild fruit.

VOCALISATION: Silent, young make a "hee-nwhe" sound.

BREEDING: 1–2 young are born from October–March. ♀ has 1–3 pairs of abdominal mammae.

AGE: ± 8 years.

WHITE-TAILED MONGOOSE *Ichneumia albicauda*
(WITSTERTMUISHOND)

Mass:	♂	±4,5 kg
	♀	±4,1 kg
Length:		± 1,1 m

IDENTIFICATION: A very large mongoose. Black legs, a long tail with long ha
which is white for the last four-fifths of its length.

DIFFERS FROM OTHER SPECIES: Selous mongoose: Smaller, and a smalle
part of the tail is white. Meller's mongoose: Sometimes has a white tail, but a brow
body.

DIFFERENCE BETWEEN ♂ AND ♀: The male is slightly heavier than the female

HABITAT: Occurs generally in well-watered woodland up to the edge of mountai
forests; also found in more arid areas along rivers and swamps such as the Okavang
delta. Prefers more humid types of woodland. Dependent on water.

HABITS: Nocturnal, active well after sunset and only until midnight. Rests durin
the day in old antbear or springhare holes. Terrestrial, seldom climbs trees, rathe
makes use of thickets or holes for shelter when chased. Usually solitary, althoug
pairs and family groups are also seen.

FOOD: Termites, beetles, locusts, crickets, frogs, mice, lizards, snakes, wild fru
and earthworms.

VOCALISATION: Unknown.

BREEDING: 1–3 young are born from September–December. ♀ has 3 pairs of ab
dominal mammae.

AGE: Unknown.

WATER MONGOOSE (Marsh mongoose) *Atilax paludinosus*
(OMMETJIEGATMUISHOND)

4,5 cm

SUBSPECIES

Only one subspecies occurs in the region.

▨ *A.p. paludinosus*

Mass: 2,4–4,1 kg

Shoulder height: ± 15 cm

IDENTIFICATION: A large mongoose. It is dark brown and has white cheeks and a large broad head. Long hair (especially on the tail).

DIFFERS FROM OTHER SPECIES: White-tailed mongoose: Lighter in colour with black legs and distinctive white tail.

DIFFERENCE BETWEEN ♂ AND ♀: None.

HABITAT: Generally found in well-watered areas – especially near rivers, dams, streams, swamps, marshes and estuaries; prefers a dense shelter in reed patches or reeds on higher ground out of reach of floodwaters. Are found in dry areas along rivers such as the Okavango Swamps and Orange River. Dependent on water.

HABITS: Mainly solitary. Active for about 2 hours before dark and 3 hours after first light, but for longer periods on overcast days. Uses paths on the muddy sides of water in search of food. Keen swimmers – takes to the water when in danger.

FOOD: Frogs, clawed frogs, crabs, marsh rats, mice, insects, insect larvae, mussels and prawns.

VOCALISATION: Growls and has a high explosive bark.

BREEDING: 1–3 young are born from August–December. ♀ has 3 pairs of abdominal mammae.

AGE: ± 11 years.

BANDED MONGOOSE *Mungos mungo*

(GEBANDE MUISHOND)

SUBSPECIES

▨ *M.m. grisonax:*
Light grey (reddish sheen) brown bands on the back

▥ *M.m. taenianotus:*
Darker, reddish-brown black bands on back

Mass: 1,0–1,6 kg

Shoulder height: ± 12,5 cm

IDENTIFICATION: Characteristic feature is the dark, transverse bands from mi back to base of tail.

DIFFERENCE BETWEEN ♂ AND ♀: None.

HABITAT: Prefers areas along rivers and marshes, as well as dry thornveld and oth thickets with sufficient trees, undergrowth, fallen logs and anthills. Fond of riverir forests along the Zambezi, Limpopo and other large rivers. Independent of water.

HABITS: Forms colonies varying from a few animals up to 30 or more. Move f apart when foraging but maintain contact by continuous twittering. All freeze an some stand on their hindlegs when an alarm call is given. Although terrestrial the sometimes take shelter in trees. Diurnal and sleep in old antbear holes or holes i anthills.

FOOD: Insects, insect larvae, millipedes, snails, lizards, frogs, scorpions, spider snakes, locusts, bird eggs and chickens, beetles, crickets, ants and wild fruit. Drink water when available.

VOCALISATION: Twittering and a loud crack sound as alarm call.

BREEDING: 2–8 young are born from October–February after a gestation perio of ± 8 weeks. ♀ has 3 pairs of abdominal mammae.

AGE: ± 8 years.

DWARF MONGOOSE *Helogale parvula*
(WERGMUISHOND)

SUBSPECIES

▨ *H.p. parvula:*
Dark brown

▧ *H.p. nero:* Black

▨ *H.p. mimetra:*
Lighter, rusty brown

Mass: 210–340 g

**Shoulder
height:** ± 7,5 cm

IDENTIFICATION: A very small mongoose. At a distance the colour seems dark-brown or black, but from nearby one can see its white speckles.

DIFFERENCE BETWEEN ♂ AND ♀: None.

HABITAT: A savannah species. Prefers dry open woodland or grassveld in which there are areas of hard or stony soil containing fallen trees, anthills and other plant material. Anthills are essential as they are used for shelter. Independent of water.

HABITS: Diurnal, becomes active long after sunrise and returns to its sleeping site long before sunset. Lives in groups of 8–10, but groups of up to 30 have been spotted. An anthill is usually the permanent shelter of such a group. They sometimes dig their own hole, placing the entrance beneath a fallen log. Keep contact with one another while foraging by constantly making "chuck" sounds.

FOOD: Insects, insect larvae, termites, snails, locusts, crickets, scorpions, centipedes, caterpillars, earthworms, lizards, snakes, mice and moth larvae.

VOCALISATION: "Perrip" and "chuck" sounds to keep contact. Alarm call is a shu-shwee" sound.

BREEDING: 2–4 young are born from October–March after a gestation period of 18 weeks. ♀ has 3 pairs of abdominal mammae.

AGE: ± 6 years.

AARDWOLF *Proteles cristatus*

(AARDWOLF)

5,5 cm

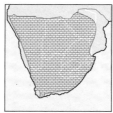

SUBSPECIES

Only one subspecies occurs in the region.

▨ *P.c. cristatus*

Mass: 7,7–13,5 kg

Shoulder height: ± 50 cm

IDENTIFICATION: Has a sloping back, 4–5 transverse black stripes on the flank and a few stripes on the legs. Has a mane of long hair.

DIFFERS FROM OTHER SPECIES: Brown hyaena: Larger, darker in colour and lacks the stripes on the flanks. Spotted hyaena: Larger, has spots and no stripes.

DIFFERENCE BETWEEN ♂ AND ♀: None.

HABITAT: Utilizes a large variety of plant habitats; generally found in dry areas (100–600 mm/annum). Prefers open areas such as dry marshes, grassplains and open patches around pans. Found only where there are sufficient termites.

HABITS: Nocturnal; rests during the day in old antbear or other holes that it adapts for itself. Solitary; does not take carrion, feeds mainly on termites. Roars and growls loudly and mane bristles when confronted. Dangerous canine teeth are seldom used. Uses glands above anus to mark its presence.

FOOD: Termites and other insects, with harvester termites being the most important. Sometimes feeds on spiders, moths, centipedes and ants but not on meat.

VOCALISATION: Growl ending in a sudden bark. Under stress a loud roar.

BREEDING: 2–4 young are born from September–April after a gestation period of ± 2 months.

AGE: ± 13 years.

BROWN HYAENA *Hyaena brunnea*
(BRUINHIËNA)

SUBSPECIES
None.

Mass:	♂	35–57 kg
	♀	28–48 kg
Shoulder	♂	± 79 cm
height:	♀	± 76 cm

IDENTIFICATION: Sloping back. A light brown neck, with a light brown mantle on the shoulders. The legs have lighter rings.

DIFFERS FROM OTHER SPECIES: Spotted hyaena: Ears are rounded, hair is much shorter, colour is yellowish; has dark spots. Aardwolf: Much smaller and of lighter colour with transverse stripes.

DIFFERENCE BETWEEN ♂ AND ♀: The male is larger than the female.

HABITAT: Generally found in arid areas. In Transvaal it prefers mountainous areas or dry mopani veld, and scavenges on the beach at night in Namibia. Uses shelters such as holes, branches of trees near the ground, thick shrubs or patches of grass.

HABITS: Mainly nocturnal; goes solitary but is attached to a group with a fixed territory. Rests during the day beneath shrubs or in holes. The group scent-mark their area and make use of communal dung heaps near the boundaries of their territory.

FOOD: Mainly carrion; hunts seldom but will feed on small animals such as springhares, mongooses, reptiles and ground-living birds.

VOCALISATION: Growls, snorts and yelps. Whines and squeals as a sign of submissiveness.

BREEDING: 1–5 young are born from August–November after a gestation period of ± 3 months. ♀ has 1 pair of abdominal mammae.

AGE: ± 24 years.

47

SPOTTED HYAENA (Laughing hyaena) *Crocuta crocuta*

(GEVLEKTE HIËNA)

9-12 cm

SUBSPECIES
None.

Mass: ♂ 46–79 kg
♀ 56–80 kg

**Shoulder
height:** ± 77 cm

IDENTIFICATION: Its neck and forequarters are very strong, with a sloping back. It has dark spots on the body which become duller with age.

DIFFERS FROM OTHER SPECIES: Brown hyaena: Darker in colour, with longer hair and more pointed ears. Aardwolf: Smaller with transverse stripes and no spots.

DIFFERENCE BETWEEN ♂ AND ♀: The female is slightly larger than the male.

HABITAT: Savannah species: dependent on the presence of antelope. Found in riverine-type savannah, but prefers open plains and woodland. Dependent on water.

HABITS: Usually single or 2–3 together belonging to a group of up to 12 animals occupying a territory. The group regularly scent-mark their area and make use of communal dung heaps in the territory. Males do not respect these boundaries and both male and female will ignore them if food is scarce. Females are dominant. Although they are sometimes seen during the day, they are primarily nocturnal. They are scavengers, but may also hunt in a pack.

FOOD: Eats carrion; sometimes hunts antelope such as impala and springbok.

VOCALISATION: Well-known "whoo-hoop" sound. Also awful "laughing" sounds.

BREEDING: 1–4 young are born anytime during the year (with a peak in late summer) after a gestation period of ± 3 months. ♀ has 1 pair of abdominal mammae.

AGE: ± 25 years.

HEETAH *Acinonyx jubatus*
(GLUIPERD)

SUBSPECIES

Only one subspecies
occurs in the region.

▨ *A.j. jubatus*

R.W.	Min: 12⅜"
	Max: 14½"
S.C.I.	Min: E.D.
	Max: 15"
Mass:	♂ 39–60 kg
	♀ 36–48 kg
Shoulder height:	± 86 cm

IDENTIFICATION: Slender with long legs. Small head with distinct dark stripes ("tearmarks") from the inside corner of the eyes to the mouth. Round or oval black spots over the entire body.

DIFFERS FROM OTHER SPECIES: Leopard: Sturdier, shorter legs and rosette-like spots.

DIFFERENCE BETWEEN ♂ AND ♀: The male is slightly heavier than the female.

HABITAT: A savannah species: found in fairly arid areas, but avoids thickets and riverine forests. Prefers more open woodland and plains as result of its hunting methods. The presence of prey is important. Independent of water.

HABITS: Mainly diurnal; most active at sunrise and sunset; rests when it is warm in a place with a clear view. Usually seen in pairs or alone. Males like to form groups. Home ranges overlap and although males mark their areas with urine, not all of them demonstrate territorial behaviour. Very fast, relies on its speed to overtake and catch its prey.

FOOD: Ostriches, impala, springbok and other small antelopes, calves of larger antelope, ground-living birds e.g. korhaans and guinea-fowls. Also hares and porcupines.

VOCALISATION: High-pitched bird-like call.

BREEDING: 1–5 young are born anytime during the year after a gestation period of ± 3 months. ♀ has 5–6 pairs of breast and abdominal mammae.

AGE: ± 12 years.

LEOPARD *Panthera pardus*

(LUIPERD)

SUBSPECIES

Only one subspecies
occurs in the region.

 P.p. melanotica

R.W.	Min: 15⅜"
	Max: 19"
S.C.I.	Min: 14"
	Max: 19"
Mass:	♂ 20–82 kg
	♀ 17–35 kg
Shoulder height:	± 65 cm

IDENTIFICATION: Strongly-built with a long tail. Light golden-brown with black spots and rosettes consisting of 4–6 spots arranged in a circle.

DIFFERS FROM OTHER SPECIES: Cheetah: Slender build, taller on its legs and with single spots. Characteristic "tear-marks".

DIFFERENCE BETWEEN ♂ AND ♀: The male is much larger than the female.

HABITAT: Very adaptable; occurs even in desert areas. Prefers stony hills, riverine forests, broken country, mountains and thickets. Prey and sufficient shelter such as rocks or bushes are essential. Independent of water.

HABITS: Solitary, except during mating time. Mainly nocturnal, but to a certain extent also diurnal in undisturbed areas. It marks its territory with urine and a male's territory overlaps with those of some females. A very good tree climber and is able to haul even large prey up a tree – out of reach of scavengers. Has keen senses and is very cunning and dangerous.

FOOD: From mice, dassies and bushpig to small and medium-sized antelope and calves of larger antelope. By exception big game such as kudu.

VOCALISATION: Most common is a hoarse cough. Growls, grumbles and purrs.

BREEDING: 2–3 (occasionally up to 6) young are born anytime during the year after a gestation period of ± 3 months. ♀ has 2 pairs of abdominal mammae.

AGE: ± 20 years.

⣿ION *Panthera leo*
(LEEU)

SUBSPECIES: None		
R.W.	Min:	24″
	Max:	28¾″
S.C.I.	Min:	22″
	Max:	28½″
Mass:	♂	180–240 kg
	♀	120–180 kg
Shoulder	♂	± 106 cm
height:	♀	± 91 cm

13 cm

IDENTIFICATION: Largest cat in the region. Young animals have dark rosettes and spots fading away as animal matures. The male usually has a darker mane on its head, neck and shoulders.

DIFFERENCE BETWEEN ♂ AND ♀: The male is much larger than the female. The female is without a mane.

HABITAT: Widespread in savannah and semidesert areas. Availability of especially medium-sized to large game is an important requirement. Also essential are shade for resting during the day and other shelter for stalking its prey. Independent of water.

HABITS: The only cats that form prides; each with an average of 12 members. Single nomadic lions are also seen. Mainly nocturnal, but also active during the day especially at sunrise and sunset. Pride consists of one or more males (one of them dominant), a dominant female, other females and young lions. They occupy a territory but do not necessarily wander together.

FOOD: Anything from mice to buffalo, and even young elephants; prefers blue wildebeest, impala and zebras. Usually hunts in a group at night.

VOCALISATION: Well-known "uuuh-Humph", gradually shorter and softer.

BREEDING: 1–4 (occasionally 6) cubs are born anytime during the year after a gestation period of ± 3 months. ♀ has 2 pairs of abdominal mammae.

AGE: ± 20 years.

51

CARACAL (Lynx) *Felis caracal*
(ROOIKAT)

Mass: ♂ 8,6–20 kg
♀ 4,2–14,5 kg
Shoulder height: ± 43 cm

IDENTIFICATION: A strongly-built cat with large paws. It has characteristic tassels of long darker hair on the tips of its ears.

DIFFERENCE BETWEEN ♂ AND ♀: The male is usually more heavily built than the female.

HABITAT: Occurs in a variety of habitats. Absent in forests and deserts. Sufficient shelter is of the utmost importance. Prefers open areas, e.g. frequents the open areas around vleis and pans, open woodland or grassplains. Independent of water.

HABITS: Mainly nocturnal and very seldom seen during the day; if so, early morning or late afternoon and on cool overcast days. Solitary, and meet only to mate. Although a good tree climber, lives and hunts mostly on the ground. Rests during the day. Has the ability to hide itself with very little shelter available.

FOOD: Duiker, steenbok, grysbok, bushbuck ewes, Damara dik-dik, young impala and springbok, lambs of sheep, dassies, squirrels, Cape hare, young monkeys, springhares, mongooses, moles, mice, guinea-fowls, and other ground-living birds.

VOCALISATION: Purrs, young ones chirp like a bird.

BREEDING: 2–4 (occasionally 5) young are born from October–March after a gestation period of ± 2 months. ♀ has 5 pairs of breast and abdominal mammae.

AGE: ± 11 years.

SERVAL *Felis serval*
(ERBOSKAT)

Mass: ♂ 8,6–13,5 kg
♀ 8,6–11,8 kg
Shoulder height: ± 56 cm

IDENTIFICATION: Slender cat with very long legs and large ears. Black stripes the neck that change into spots stretching in line from the front backwards.

DIFFERENCE BETWEEN ♂ AND ♀: The male is slightly heavier than the female.

HABITAT: Absent in dry areas such as deserts or semideserts. Only enters an arid ea when a river provides a suitable habitat. Prefers savannah with high rainfall, or eas containing stagnant water. Water and sufficient shelter such as thick grass, umps of bushes or reeds are important requirements.

HABITS: Mainly nocturnal and seldom seen during the day. They sometimes hunt pairs but are usually solitary. Ranges far in search of food, using footpaths on its ay to hunt to avoid difficult terrain. Hunts vlei rats in swampy areas among water-ass, where the water may be up to 8 cm deep. Not an eager tree climber, but will ke to the trees when attacked. Fast over short distances.

FOOD: Mainly vlei rats and mice. Also finches, ducks, lizards, snakes, scrub hare, ne rats and locusts. Sometimes returns to prey of previous day.

VOCALISATION: Grunts, grumbles and spits.

BREEDING: 1–4 young are born from September–April after a gestation period of 2 months. ♀ has 1 pair of groin and 2 pairs of abdominal mammae.

AGE: ± 12 years.

SMALL SPOTTED CAT (Black-footed cat) *Felis nigripes*

(KLEIN GEKOLDE KAT)

SUBSPECIES

F.n. nigripes: Light yellowish-brown, rusty brown spots and stripes

F.n. thomasi: Brownish-yellow, distinct black spots and stripes

Mass: ♂ 1,5–1,7 kg
♀ 1,0–1,4 kg
Shoulder height: ± 25 cm

IDENTIFICATION: Smallest cat of the region. Light yellowish-brown with da spots. Has dark stripes against the neck and throat.

DIFFERS FROM OTHER SPECIES: African wild cat: Larger, tawny-grey colo and without the distinct dark spots on the body.

DIFFERENCE BETWEEN ♂ AND ♀: The male is slightly more heavily built th the female.

HABITAT: Only found in more arid areas (100–500 mm/annum). Prefers open are that offer shelter, such as patches of tall grass or shrubs, to flee to. It also uses shelte such as springhare or antbear holes or holes in anthills in which to rest during t day. Independent of water.

HABITS: Nocturnal, appearing only some hours after sunset. Usually solitary, e cept in the mating season when a few males accompany a female. Lives and hun mainly on the ground, but is a good tree climber. Rests during the heat of day. S and very aggressive for its size.

FOOD: Mainly mice and spiders. Also agamas, ground-living birds and insects.

VOCALISATION: Spits and growls.

BREEDING: 1–3 young are born from November–December after a gestati period of ± 2 months.

AGE: Unknown.

AFRICAN WILD CAT *Felis lybica*

(AALBOSKAT)

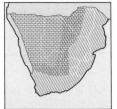

SUBSPECIES

▨ *F.l. cafra:* Darker, grey, black markings

▦ *F.l. griselda:* Lighter, sandy grey, rusty brown markings

Mass: ♂ 3,8–6,4 kg
♀ 2,6–5,5 kg

Shoulder height: ± 35 cm

IDENTIFICATION: Resembles a grey domestic cat; has long legs. Tawny-grey with dark stripes and rings on the legs and tail. Reddish behind the ears.

DIFFERS FROM OTHER SPECIES: Domestic cat or crosses between the two: shorter legs, more spots on the body and lacks the reddishness behind the ears. Small spotted cat: Smaller and lighter in colour with distinct spots on the body.

DIFFERENCE BETWEEN ♂ AND ♀: The male is more heavily built than the female.

HABITAT: Widespread except in mountain forests and deserts. Requires shelter such as rocky slopes, dense bush, reeds or tall grass, antbear holes or holes in anthills for resting in during the day. Independent of water.

HABITS: Mainly solitary and nocturnal, appears only after sunset. Although a good tree climber, it lives predominantly on the ground. Territorial, with both male and female marking and defending their area. They like to use the same footpaths. Crossbreeds easily with the domestic cat.

FOOD: Mice, vlei rats, rats, ducks, chickens, doves, bustards, lizards, snakes, hares, springhares, spiders, frogs and wild fruit.

VOCALISATION: Groans, hisses, growls and spits.

BREEDING: 2–5 young are born anytime of the year, gestation period ± 2 months.

AGE: Unknown.

ELEPHANT *Loxodonta africana*

(OLIFANT)

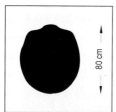

SUBSPECIES

Only one subspecies
occurs in the region.

▨ *L.a. africana*

R.W.	Min: 80 lb
	Max: 226 lb
S.C.I.	Min: 100 lb
	Max: 228 lb
Record length:	11'5"
Mass:	♂ 5500–6000 k
	♀ 3600–4000 k
Shoulder height:	± 3,5 m

IDENTIFICATION: Huge animal with long thick legs and very large ears. Its trur
is versatile acting as nose and hand. Usually has long tusks.

DIFFERENCE BETWEEN♂AND♀: The bull is larger than the cow and has large
and heavier tusks.

HABITAT: Found in areas ranging from the arid Kaokoland to dense savannah re
cording a high rainfall. Clear drinking water, other permanent water, shade an
enough food (grass and branches) are essential. Dependent on water.

HABITS: Diurnal and nocturnal. Gregarious; herds consist mainly of a cow and he
descendants. Bulls form temporary male herds or live alone (especially the old ones
only joining the cows for mating. Large breeding herds with bulls also exist. It show
aggression when it lifts its trunk and head, spreads out its ears and trumpets, or kick
up dust. When drinking water it squirts it over itself or lies down to cool off. Enjoy
wallowing in mud, and rubbing against trees.

FOOD: Branches, grass, leaves, bark and fruit. May drink water once in four day
or even daily. Water for drinking must be clear – may even dig in the sand.

VOCALISATION: Screams and trumpets. Keeps contact by deep rumbling.

BREEDING: 1, rarely 2, calves are born at any time during the year after a gestatio
period of ± 22 months. ♀ has 1 pair of mammae between the front legs.

AGE: ± 65 years.

MOUNTAIN ZEBRA *Equus zebra*
(BERGKWAGGA)

SUBSPECIES

▮ *E.z. zebra:* Broader stripes on buttocks

▮ *E.z. hartmannae:* Larger, narrower stripes on buttocks

Cape mountain zebra

Hartmanns mountain zebra

Mass: ♂ 250–330 kg
♀ 204–300 kg

Shoulder height: ± 126–150 cm

IDENTIFICATION: Horse-like animal with a dewlap and black stripes ending down the flanks, leaving the belly white and extending down the legs to the hooves.

DIFFERS FROM OTHER SPECIES: Burchell's zebra: Without dewlap, stripes continue on to the belly; there are shadow stripes on the white stripes.

DIFFERENCE BETWEEN ♂ AND ♀: The male is slightly larger than the female.

HABITAT: Restricted to mountainous areas containing their preferential grazing, water and ravines for shelter against cold winds. Prefers plateaus and mountain slopes. *E.z. hartmannae* moves seasonally downhill for grazing. Dependent on water.

HABITS: Diurnal, active during the cooler parts of the day and rests when it is warm. Gregarious with herds consisting mainly of a dominant stallion, mares and foals. Mares usually spend their whole lives in the same herd. Some stallions move on their own while others form male herds. From time to time younger stallions challenge the dominant stallions in the breeding herd to depose them.

FOOD: Mainly grass, but occasionally also shrubs and twigs. Drinks water regularly (at least once a day).

VOCALISATION: Snorts and a shrill alarm call.

BREEDING: 1 foal is born anytime during the year after a gestation period of ± 12 months. ♀ has 1 pair of groin mammae.   **AGE:** ± 35 years.

57

BURCHELL'S ZEBRA *Equus burchelli*
(BONTKWAGGA)

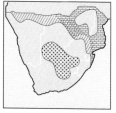

SUBSPECIES

- *E.b. burchelli:* Extinct
- *E.b. antiquorum:* Lacks stripes lower down the legs
- *E.b. chapmani:* Stripes go down to the hooves

Mass: ♂ 290–340 kg
♀ 290–325 kg
Shoulder height: ± 134 cm

IDENTIFICATION: Horse-like animal. The stripes on the flanks continue on to the belly. There are dull shadow stripes on the white stripes. Lower down towards the hooves the stripes become indistinct.

DIFFERS FROM OTHER SPECIES: Mountain zebra: It has a dewlap, legs are striped to the hooves, belly is white and it does not have the shadow stripes.

DIFFERENCE BETWEEN ♂ AND ♀: Stallion slightly heavier than mare.

HABITAT: A savannah species: prefers open woodland, grassveld and floodplains. Avoids dense savannah and is seldom seen further than 12 km from water. Ranges in search of grazing areas but availability of water is the determinant.

HABITS: Gregarious: forms herds consisting of a stallion, one or more mares and their offspring. Other stallions form male herds or go on their own. Fond of dust baths. In some areas they move over large distances from winter to summer grazing areas – leaving the summer grazing area just before the seasonal water supply dries up.

FOOD: Mainly grass, sometimes leaves, branches and pods. Drinks water regularly.

VOCALISATION: A "qua-ha-ha" whinny followed by a whistling sound when air is inhaled; this is repeated a few times.

BREEDING: A single foal is born anytime during the year (peak in summer) after a gestation period of ± 12 months. ♀ has 1 pair of groin mammae.

AGE: ± 35 years.

WHITE RHINOCEROS (Square-lipped rhinoceros) *Ceratotherium simum*
(WITRENOSTER)

23–28 cm

SUBSPECIES
Only one subspecies occurs in the region.

▨ *C.s. simum*

R.W.	Min: 28″
	Max: 62¼″
S.C.I.	Min: 70″
	Max: 111⅜″
Mass:	♂ 2000–2300 kg
	♀ 1400–1600 kg
Shoulder height:	± 170 cm

IDENTIFICATION: Huge animal with an elongated head and two horns on the snout. Mouth is square and wide.

DIFFERS FROM OTHER SPECIES: Black rhinoceros: Smaller with a prehensile upper lip and shorter head. Has no hump on the neck. Walks with head held high.

DIFFERENCE BETWEEN ♂ AND ♀: The bull is heavier than the cow.

HABITAT: Wooded grassplains with open marshes and enough water. Important requirements include areas with short grass, availability of water to drink as well as water to bathe in, thickets for shelter and fairly flat terrain.

HABITS: Lives in small groups consisting of a territorial bull, other bulls (tolerated by him), cows and young ones. A territorial bull sprays urine and defecates in latrines along boundaries as way of marking its territory. Only the territorial bull urinates by spraying through its hindlegs, the others urinate normally. The territories of territorial bulls become larger in dry season, while the home ranges of cows overlap. Poor eyesight but acute senses of hearing and smell. The calf usually walks in front of its mother.

FOOD: Grass, especially short grass. Drinks water when available.

VOCALISATION: Pants to keep contact. Blows, snorts, yells and growls.

BREEDING: Single calf is born anytime during the year after a gestation period of ± 16 months. ♀ has 1 pair of groin mammae.

AGE: ± 45 years.

BLACK RHINOCEROS (Hook-lipped rhinoceros) *Diceros bicornis*
(SWARTRENOSTER)

R.W.	Min: 24″
	Max: 47¼″
S.C.I.	Min: 56″
	Max: 89½″
Mass:	♂ 730–970 kg
	♀ 760–1000 kg
Shoulder height:	± 160 cm

IDENTIFICATION: Huge animal. Two horns on top of the snout and the prehensile upperlip is pointed. Sometimes has bloody skin lesions caused by parasites.

DIFFERS FROM OTHER SPECIES: White rhinoceros: Larger with elongated head, a hump on the neck and a square mouth. Walks with head close to the ground.

DIFFERENCE BETWEEN ♂ AND ♀: The cow is slightly heavier than the bull.

HABITAT: Woodland with thickets for shelter and water to drink and bathe in. Shrubs and trees of up to 4 metres are essential for browsing (will even push down trees to reach leaves). Dependent on water, seldom further than 15 km from water.

HABITS: Solitary. Although the bulls spray urine on bushes and have dung heaps they are not territorial animals as home ranges overlap. Bulls fight over a cow in oestrus and not over territory. Aggressive; although it avoids contact, serious fights do occur. Rests in shade or wallows in the mud when it is hot. The calf usually walks behind its mother.

FOOD: Leaves, small branches, sticks and thorns. When available, drinks water daily, usually at night. Sometimes digs in the sand if water has dried up.

VOCALISATION: Snorts, screams and growls. Cows call calves with a "mewing" sound.

BREEDING: Single calf is born anytime during the year after a gestation period of ± 15 months. ♀ has 1 pair of groin mammae.

AGE: ± 40 years.

60

OCK DASSIE (Stone badger) *Procavia capensis*
(PDASSIE)

3.5 cm

SUBSPECIES

None.

Mass: ♂ 3,2–4,7 kg
♀ 2,5–4,2 kg
**Shoulder
height:** ± 25 cm

IDENTIFICATION: Small sturdy animal with short legs and no tail. On the back a patch of black hair.

DIFFERS FROM OTHER SPECIES: Yellow-spotted rock dassie: Slightly smaller, patch on the back is yellow and the spots above the eyes are white. Tree dassie: ear is longer than that of the other two species and the patch on the back is white.

DIFFERENCE BETWEEN ♂ AND ♀: The male is slightly heavier than the female.

HABITAT: Rocky area with crevices, caves or holes for shelter as well as shrubs and/or trees. Found usually on a stony hill, cliff and even small stone heaps where yellow-spotted dassies do not occur.

HABITS: Gregarious, lives in colonies that could number a few hundred with a definite hierarchy. Often lives together with yellow-spotted dassies. Mainly diurnal. Forages early in the morning and late in the afternoon – even well into the night if there is sufficient moonlight. On cold mornings it first warms itself by sitting in the sun, while a female stands sentry. Uses fixed latrine places.

FOOD: Grass, herbs, shrubs and other leaves.

VOCALISATION: Sharp alarm bark, snorts, screams, growls and chirps.

BREEDING: 1–6 young are born in Sept./Oct. (winter rainfall areas) and March–April (summer rainfall areas) after a gestation period of ± 7 months.

AGE: ± 6 years.

61

ANTBEAR (Aardvark) *Orycteropus afer*

(ERDVARK)

SUBSPECIES

Only one subspecies occurs in the region.

 O.a. afer

Mass: ♂ 41–65 kg
♀ 40–58 kg
**Shoulder
height:** ± 61 cm

IDENTIFICATION: Hindquarters are much heavier than the forequarters. Has elongated pig-like snout, long ears and a thick tapering tail.

DIFFERENCE BETWEEN ♂ AND ♀: The male is slightly heavier than the fema

HABITAT: Prefers open woodland (dry islands in Okavango Swamps), grassla or shrubby areas. Although it seems to prefer sandy soil, it is also found on mo clayish soil such as that found in mopane veld. The availability of termites is a dete minant. Independent of water.

HABITS: Solitary, mainly nocturnal. Sleeps during the day in a hole, after it h closed the entrance only appears late at night. Travels long distances in search of fo with its nose held close to the ground. Acute senses of smell and hearing, but po eyesight. There are three types of holes: permanent burrows containing several tu nels and entrances, semipermanent shelters, and diggings made in search of food th are not used again. The tongue is very sticky and is used to catch termites and an

FOOD: Mainly termites and ants.

VOCALISATION: Grunts and snuffles, otherwise silent.

BREEDING: A single young is born from July–September after a gestation peri of ± 7 months.

AGE: ± 10 years.

WARTHOG *Phacochoerus aethiopicus*
(AKVARK)

5,5 cm

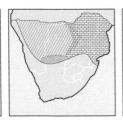

SUBSPECIES

▨ *P.a. aethiopicus*
▦ *P.a. sundevalli*
▨ *P.a. shortridgei*

R.W.	Min: 13″
	Max: 24″
S.C.I.	Min: 30″
	Max: 49⅞″
Mass:	♂ 60–100 kg
	♀ 45–70 kg
Shoulder	♂ ± 70 cm
height:	♀ ± 60 cm

IDENTIFICATION: Snout is broader than that of a domestic pig and long canine teeth curl over the snout. Lifts its tail vertically when it runs away.

DIFFERS FROM OTHER SPECIES: Bushpig: Brown with a lighter mane, a narrower snout, smaller canine teeth and usually no warts.

DIFFERENCE BETWEEN ♂ AND ♀: The male has two pairs of warts and the female only one pair. The male is appreciably larger and has longer canine teeth.

HABITAT: Areas with short grass and mud pools. Prefers open woodland, grassplains (especially floodplains), vleis and open areas surrounding pans and water holes. Likes areas where fresh grass grows following a fire. Avoids thickets. Independent of water.

HABITS: Lives in family groups (male, female and her young), nursing groups (one or more females and their young) and temporary male groups, while solitary males are not uncommon. Diurnal and sleeps at night in old antbear holes that it enters backwards. Such holes also serve as a shelter against predators and bad weather. Home ranges overlap and become larger in dry seasons. Likes to wallow in the mud.

FOOD: Grass, rhizomes and wild fruit. Drinks water regularly when available.

VOCALISATION: Growls, snorts and grunts. The male snaps its jaws as an overture to mating.

BREEDING: 1–8 young are born from Sept.–Dec. after a gestation period of ± 5 months. ♀ has 2 pairs of groin mammae.   **AGE:** ± 20 years.

63

BUSHPIG *Potamochoerus porcus*

(BOSVARK)

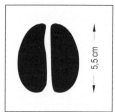

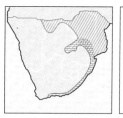

R.W.	Min: 3⅞"
	Max: 11⅞"
S.C.I.	Min: 11"
	Max: 22⅜"
Mass:	♂ 46–82 kg
	♀ 48–66 kg
Shoulder height:	± 75 cm

IDENTIFICATION: Resembles the domestic pig. Predominantly brown with mane of lighter hair. The young have horizontal white stripes on their bodies.

DIFFERS FROM OTHER SPECIES: Warthog: Greyer, with larger canine teeth a broad snout and warts on the face.

DIFFERENCE BETWEEN ♂ AND ♀: The male is usually heavier than the female

HABITAT: Thick shelter and water are essential. Prefers coastal, mountainous an riverine forests, thickets, reed patches and tall grass near water. Found only unde these conditions even in dry country.

HABITS: Lives in groups of 7 animals (even up to 12), consisting of a dominan male, dominant female, other females and young. Groups with young are very ag gressive. Mainly nocturnal, but diurnal in areas where it is protected. Forages a night, tramping out footpaths. Digs in the soil just like warthogs, and likes to wallov in the mud to cool down.

FOOD: Digs in soft soil for rhizomes, bulbs and tubers. Also eats earthworms, ve getables, chickens, leaves and wild fruit that have fallen.

VOCALISATION: Groans while eating. Alarm call is a long protracted growl.

BREEDING: 3–8 young are born from November–January after a gestation perio of ± 4 months. ♀ has 3 pairs of abdominal mammae.

AGE: ± 20 years.

HIPPOPOTAMUS *Hippopotamus amphibius*
(EEKOEI)

22–25 cm

SUBSPECIES

▒ *H.a. Capensis*
▓ *H.a. Constrictus*

R.W.	Min: 29⅞″
	Max: 64½″
S.C.I.	Min: 50″
	Max: 88⅝″
Mass:	♂ 970–2000 kg
	♀ 995–1675 kg
Shoulder	♂ ± 150 cm
height:	♀ ± 144 cm

IDENTIFICATION: Very large barrel-shaped body and short legs. Skin is naked and predominantly greyish-brown, but yellowish-pink against the throat, belly and some skin folds.

DIFFERENCE BETWEEN ♂ AND ♀: The male is larger than the female.

HABITAT: Open stretches of permanent water or riverine pools with gently sloping sandbanks for resting on. The area should contain enough food. Prefers pools that are deep enough for submersion, with slow running water. Moves away during floods but returns to the same pools if they have not changed much.

HABITS: Grazes at night. Rests during the day, half-submerged or on a sandbank if it is not too hot. Sometimes grazes far from water, especially during dry periods. Makes use of the same route frequently and leaves a double-track game path. Gregarious, with herds consisting of 10–15 animals. If pools with sufficient water become scarce towards the end of winter, larger numbers of animals flock together. Although an adult male leads the group to grazing areas at night, there is a definite hierarchy with a cow as the leader.

FOOD: Grass – 130 kg in order to be satiated.

VOCALISATION: A high roaring bellow followed by 5 short ones at a lower pitch.

BREEDING: A single young is born anytime during the year after a gestation period of 7–8 months. ♀ has 1 pair of groin mammae.   **AGE:** ± 39 years.

GIRAFFE *Giraffa camelopardalis*
(KAMEELPERD)

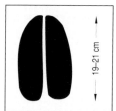

19-21 cm

SUBSPECIES

▨ *G.c. capensis*

▨ *G.c. angolensis*

Mass: ♂ 970–1395 kg
             ♀ 700–950 kg
**Shoulder
height:** ± 300 cm

IDENTIFICATION: Unmistakable long neck and legs. Light brown patches on yellowish to white background. It has two short horns on the head.

DIFFERENCE BETWEEN ♂ AND ♀: The male is usually heavier than the female

HABITAT: Occurs in a variety of plant habitats. Found in dry types of woodland from low shrubveld to fairly dense woodland. An important requirement is the presence of the different plants on which it feeds throughout the year, especially different kinds of thorn trees. Avoids dense bush. Independent of water.

HABITS: Mainly diurnal. Rests standing or lying down during the heat of the day with its head held upright. Sleeps with the head bending backwards against the body. Gregarious with loose associations – individuals wander between herds. Herds consist of females and their young, but there are also herds consisting of males, females and young. Although most adult males go single, younger males form male herds that have a hierarchy. Males fight using their heads to hit one another.

FOOD: Mainly leaves, especially of thorn trees in the wet season and of evergreen trees in dry season. Drinks water regularly when available.

VOCALISATION: Snorts or grunts when alarmed, bellows when hungry.

BREEDING: A single young is born anytime during the year after a gestation period of ± 15 months. ♀ has 2 pairs of groin mammae.

AGE: ± 28 years.

BLACK WILDEBEEST (White-tailed gnu) *Connochaetes gnou*
(SWARTWILDEBEES)

7,5-9,5 cm

SUBSPECIES

None.

R.W.	Min: 22⅞″
	Max: 29⅜″
S.C.I.	Min: 50″
	Max: 95½″
Mass:	♂ ± 180 kg
	♀ ± 140 kg
Shoulder	♂ ± 120 cm
height:	♀ ± 110 cm

IDENTIFICATION: Cattle-like, appears to be sulky, characteristic beard, hair on the nose. Distinctive long, almost white horse's tail. Horns: Both male and female.

DIFFERS FROM OTHER SPECIES: Blue wildebeest: Larger, the horns bent sideways, and has a black tail. Not found in the Highveld.

DIFFERENCE BETWEEN ♂ AND ♀: The male is larger than the female.

HABITAT: Found in open plains with water; grassplains of the OFS and Transvaal Highveld. In the past occurred in abundance in the Karroo areas of the northern, central and north-eastern Cape Province. Dependent on water.

HABITS: Gregarious; female herds, bachelor herds and territorial males can be distinguished. A territorial male is closely attached to its territory throughout the year, marking it with urine and glandular excretions; it is the only male that mates. Female herds are allowed to pass freely through his territory. Threatening behaviour: pawing or horning the ground and kneeling, serious fights are rare. Herds are active early in the morning and late in the afternoon. They rest during the heat of the day and these resting periods become shorter during winter.

FOOD: Grass, also Karroo bushes. Drinks water regularly, mainly in the late afternoon.

VOCALISATION: Snorts and a loud "ghe-nu" sound by territorial males.

BREEDING: A single young is born from December–January after a gestation period of ± 8 months. ♀ has 1 pair of groin mammae.   **AGE:** ± 20 years.

BLUE WILDEBEEST (Brindled gnu) *Connochaetes taurinus*
(BLOUWILDEBEES)

SUBSPECIES

Only one subspecies
occurs in the region.

 C.t. taurinus

R.W.	Min: 28½″
	Max: 33⅞″
S.C.I.	Min: 70″
	Max: 99⅝″
Mass:	♂ 230–270 kg
	♀ 160–200 kg
Shoulder	♂ ± 150 cm
height:	♀ ± 135 cm

IDENTIFICATION: Cattle-like animal – the face, mane and horse's tail are black. Dark vertical stripes on the neck and flanks. Both males and females have horns.

DIFFERS FROM OTHER SPECIES: Black wildebeest: Smaller with horns curving forward and upwards and a white tail. Absent in savanna.

DIFFERENCE BETWEEN ♂ AND ♀: The male is larger than the female.

HABITAT: Open savanna, especially thorn and tambotie woodland. Prefers short grassplains in valleys and floodplains. Seasonal movements take place to areas with short grass if the grass in the particular area becomes too tall. Dependent on water.

HABITS: Usually forms herds of between 20 and 30 animals. There are female and bachelor herds as well as territorial males with female herds forming the closest association. Female herds may move through a male's territory. Bachelor herds have a loose association. Grazes when it is cool and rests during the hottest part of the day in the shade. Settled in certain areas but migrates seasonally to other areas, forming larger herds numbering thousands.

FOOD: Mainly short grass of up to 15 cm. Sometimes also bark and leaves.

VOCALISATION: Snorts, bellows and grunts. Small ones bleat; young ones make a "hunn" sound.

BREEDING: 1 (occasionally 2) young are born from November–February after a gestation period of ± 8 months. ♀ has 1 pair of groin mammae. **AGE:** ± 20 years.

ICHTENSTEIN'S HARTEBEEST   *Sigmoceros lichtensteinii*
(OFHARTBEES)

SUBSPECIES	
None.	

R.W.	Min: 18½″
	Max: 24⅜″
S.C.I.	Min: 53″
	Max: 73″
Mass:	♂ 157–204 kg
	♀ 160–181 kg
Shoulder	♂ ± 129 cm
height:	♀ ± 124 cm

IDENTIFICATION: The shins and the tuft of long hair on the tail are black. The dark patch behind the shoulders is caused by the animal rubbing its horns and face here after horning the ground. Both males and females have horns.

DIFFERS FROM OTHER SPECIES: Red hartebeest: Darker reddish-brown. The upper legs and the blaze on the face are black. Tsessebe: Darker with black blaze and legs. Horns wider.

DIFFERENCE BETWEEN ♂ AND ♀: The male is slightly larger than the female.

HABITAT: A savannah species. Prefers the strips of grassveld between vleis (or floodplains) and the surrounding woodland that contain enough water and sufficient perennial types of grass. Dependent on water.

HABITS: Gregarious; herds of 3–12 animals consisting of a territorial male, some females and their offspring. Other males either go single or form herds. The territorial male keeps a distance from his females and watches the vicinity from high places such as anthills. He marks his territory by creating latrines and by rubbing the pre-orbital glands on the ground. Acute sense of sight but poor sense of smell.

FOOD: Mainly grass, especially fresh sprouts. Drinks water regularly.

VOCALISATION: Bellows or a sneezing-snort when alarmed.

BREEDING: A single young is born from June–September after a gestation period of ± 8 months. ♀ has 1 pair of groin mammae.   **AGE:** Unknown.

69

RED HARTEBEEST (Cape hartebeest) *Alcelaphus buselaphus*

(ROOIHARTBEES)

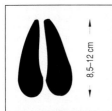

8,5–12 cm

R.W.	Min: 23″
	Max: 29½″
S.C.I.	Min: 62″
	Max: 80⅜″
Mass:	♂ 137–180 kg
	♀ 105–136 kg
Shoulder	♂ ± 125 cm
height:	♀ ± 119 cm

IDENTIFICATION: Glossy reddish-brown. The tail, blaze on the face and the ou side of the legs are black. The male and female have horns.

DIFFERS FROM OTHER SPECIES: Lichtenstein's hartebeest: Lighter in colou The shins of the legs are black and the horns further apart at the base. Tsessebe: Horn are different and the black against the legs ends further up.

DIFFERENCE BETWEEN ♂ AND ♀: The male is larger than the female.

HABITAT: Found in semidesert savannah. May occur in open woodland but avoid dense woodland. Prefers open plains such as grassplains, floodplains, grassveld, vle and the strips of grass around pans. Independent of water.

HABITS: Gregarious; forms herds of up to 20 animals. Mass herds of some thou sands have been seen in Botswana. Territorial males, harem herds, bachelor herd and solitary males exist. Harem herds are stable and consist of a territorial male the leader, young males, females and their offspring. Active in the early mornin and late afternoons; lies in the sun to rest except when it is very hot.

FOOD: Grass, especially red-grass also leaves. Drinks when water is available.

VOCALISATION: Sneezing-snorting sound as an alarm.

BREEDING: A single young is born from October–December after a gestatio period of ± 8 months. ♀ has 1 pair of groin mammae.

AGE: ± 13 years.

ONTEBOK/BLESBOK *Damaliscus dorcas*

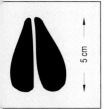

SUBSPECIES

D.d. dorcas: Larger white patches especially on the croup

D.d. phillipsi: Smaller white patches, the small and large blaze on the face are usually divided

ntebok   Blesbok

R.W.	Min: 14″/15½″
	Max: 16¾″/20″
S.C.I.	Min: 36″/39″
	Max: 47⅝″/52⅛″
Massa:	♂ ± 64/70 kg
	♀ ± 59/61 kg
Shoulder height:	± 90/95cm

DENTIFICATION: Distinct white blaze on the face. The belly, inner parts of the ttocks and the legs below the knee are white. The male and female have horns.

IFFERENCE BETWEEN ♂ **AND** ♀: The male is slightly larger than the female d its horns are thicker.

ABITAT: Grassplains with sufficient drinking water and cover. Blesbok prefers veet grassplains. Bontebok lives in a coastal plain in the Cape fynbos area that conins plenty of grass and shrubs for cover.

ABITS: Diurnal; grazing in the early morning and late afternoon, resting in the shade hen it is hot. Walk in single file between drinking and feeding places. Gregarious; there e territorial males, female herds and bachelor herds. Territories are maintained by chalnging displays, threatening behaviour and marking of grass with the pre-orbital glands. rritorial males make use of common dung heaps and sometimes lie down on top of em to rest. Blesbok's territorial behaviour becomes less marked and herd structures ange after the mating season, while those of the Bontebok remain unchanged.

OOD: Grass, especially short or in burnt areas. Drinks water regularly.

OCALISATION: Snorts and growls.

REEDING: A single young is born from September–November (bontebok) and ovember–January (blesbok) after a gestation period of ± 8 months. ♀ has 1 pair of oin mammae.   **AGE:** ± 11 years.

71

TSESSEBE (Sassaby) *Damaliscus lunatus*
(BASTERHARTBEES)

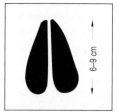

R.W.	Min: 15″
	Max: 18½″
S.C.I.	Min: 40″
	Max: 55½″
Mass:	♂ 140 kg
	♀ 126 kg
Shoulder	♂ ± 126 cm
height:	♀ ± 125 cm

IDENTIFICATION: Dark reddish-brown with a metallic sheen. The blaze on t face, buttocks, shoulders and upper legs is black. The male and female have horn

DIFFERS FROM OTHER SPECIES: Red hartebeest: A redder colour. Horns a closer at the base. Lichtenstein's hartebeest: Yellowish-brown, without black blaze and upperlegs.

DIFFERENCE BETWEEN ♂ AND ♀: The male is heavier than the female.

HABITAT: Prefers open areas on the edge of grassplains with woodland. Mediu to tall tasty grass, shade and water are important requirements. Makes temporary u of areas containing only seasonal water.

HABITS: Fastest antelope of the region. Gregarious; forms herds of 2–30 whi larger herds are also known. There are territorial males, breeding herds and bachel herds. A territorial male regularly patrols its borders marking them with droppin and manoeuvering the grass stems into its pre-orbital glands. Enjoys horning t ground. In mating season gathers a harem in his area, taking over the leadership a expelling the young males in the herd.

FOOD: Grass. Drinks water regularly.

VOCALISATION: Snorts.

BREEDING: A single young is born from September–November after a gestatic period of ± 8 months. ♀ has 1 pair of groin mammae.   **AGE:** ± 15 years.

BLUE DUIKER *Cephalophus monticola*
(BLOUDUIKER)

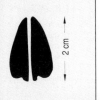

SUBSPECIES

▨ *C.m. monticola:*
Dark brown body,
tail white underneath

▧ *C.m. bicolor:* Upper
parts reddish-brown

▦ *C.m. hecki:* Upper
parts rust brown,
neck greyish-brown

R.W.	Min: 1¾″
	Max: 2⅞″
S.C.I.	Min: 4″
	Max: 8⅝″
Mass:	♂ 3,8–5,5 kg
	♀ 4,6–7,3 kg
Shoulder	♂ ± 30 cm
height:	♀ ± 31,5 cm

IDENTIFICATION: Smallest antelope of the region. Greyish-brown with a slight blueish sheen on its back. The throat, chest and belly are of lighter colour, almost white. The male and female have horns.

DIFFERS FROM OTHER SPECIES: Red duiker: Larger and more reddish.

DIFFERENCE BETWEEN ♂ AND ♀: The female is slightly larger than the male.

HABITAT: Limited to very dense coastal and other forests. Although it grazes in the more open areas in the forest, it requires patches of dense undergrowth so that it can flee or rest during the day. Dependent on water.

HABITS: Solitary. Forages in the early morning and from late afternoon until about 22:00. Forages in more open areas and at night even at the edge of the forest. Very wary and flees to dense undergrowth at the slightest sign of danger. Always alert when nearing an open patch in the forest; it hesitates – making very sure there is no danger before going further. Tramps definite footpaths in the forest between resting places and foraging or drinking places.

FOOD: Leaves, wild fruit (dropped by monkeys) and small branches. Drinks water regularly.

VOCALISATION: A piercing alarm whistle. Loud "mew", like a cat, when in danger.

BREEDING: A single young is born anytime during the year after a gestation period of ± 4 months. ♀ has 2 pairs of groin mammae. **AGE:** ± 7 years.

73

RED DUIKER (Natal duiker)   *Cephalophus natalensis*

(ROOIDUIKER)

2,5 cm

SUBSPECIES

▨ *C.n. natalensis:*
Upper parts dark
orange-red, under
parts lighter

▨ *C.n robertsi:* Upper
parts more orange,
under parts lighter

R.W.	Min: 2½″
	Max: 4⅛″
S.C.I.	Min: 8″
	Max: 12⅝″
Mass:	11–14 kg
Shoulder	
height:	± 43 cm

IDENTIFICATION: A distinct deep chestnut-red. A tuft of long darker hair between the horns. The male and female both have horns.

DIFFERS FROM OTHER SPECIES: Blue duiker: Smaller and greyish-brown colour.

DIFFERENCE BETWEEN ♂ AND ♀: None.

HABITAT: Confined to thickets and forests with well-developed undergrowth. Dependent on water. Limited to dense mountainous forest, riverine forest, wooded ravines and coastal forest with water.

HABITS: Solitary, although pairs or a female with her young are also seen. Very timid and is seldom seen except on cool, cloudy days. Takes flight to denser areas the slightest sign of danger. Likes to forage beneath trees where samango monkeys have dropped fruit. Uses communal dung heaps. May be territorial.

FOOD: Fresh and dry leaves, small branches and wild fruit. Drinks water regularly.

VOCALISATION: A loud "chee-chee" sound (louder than that of a suni) and whistling screaming sound.

BREEDING: A single young is born anytime during the year. ♀ has 2 pairs of groin mammae.

AGE: ± 12 years.

OMMON DUIKER (Grey duiker) *Sylvicapra grimmia*
UIKER)

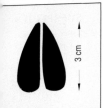

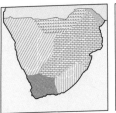

SUBSPECIES

▓	*S.g. grimmia*
▥	*S.g. burchelli*
▦	*S.g. caffra*
▨	*S.g. steinhardti*
▥	*S.g. orbicularis*
▦	*S.g. splendidula*

R.W.	Min:	4½″
	Max:	7⅛″
S.C.I.	Min:	11″
	Max:	17⅜″
Mass:	♂	15–21 kg
	♀	17–25 kg
Shoulder	♂	± 50 cm
height:	♀	± 52 cm

DENTIFICATION: A black stripe on the snout from the forehead to the nose.

IFFERS FROM OTHER SPECIES: Red duiker: Somewhat smaller and more ·ddish.

IFFERENCE BETWEEN ♂ AND ♀: Only the male has horns.

ABITAT: Prefers woodland with sufficient undergrowth and thickets. Important ·quirements are thickets, shrubs or tall grass on which it feeds, and in which it takes ·helter when in danger and to rest. Avoids open woodland, short grassveld and dense ·ountain or coastal forests. Independent of water.

ABITS: Solitary, except in the mating season. Forages in the early mornings and ·te afternoons until after dark. Active for longer periods on cool cloudy days. More ·octurnal outside conservation areas. Lies down in dense shelter, underneath shrubs ·r in tall grass during the hottest part of the day to rest. Waits until the last moment ·efore running away, head down and with characteristic jumping and swerving ·ovements. Acute senses of smell and sight.

OOD: Leaves, small branches, fruit, flowers, seed and vegetables. Seldom drinks ·ater.

OCALISATION: A nasal snort as an alarm call. Loud scream when in danger.

REEDING: 1 (seldom 2) young are born anytime during the year after a gestation ·eriod of ± 3 months. ♀ has 2 pairs of groin mammae.   **AGE:** ± 10 years.

75

SPRINGBOK *Antidorcas marsupialis*

(SPRINGBOK)

R.W.	Min: 14″
	Max: 19⅜″
S.C.I.	Min: 30″
	Max: 50⅞″
Mass:	♂ 33–48 kg
	♀ 30–44 kg
Shoulder height:	± 75 cm

IDENTIFICATION: Distinct dark-brown stripes on the flanks above the whi belly. White face with dark stripes from the eyes to the mouth. ♂ and ♀ have horn

DIFFERS FROM OTHER SPECIES: Impala: Larger, more reddish brown, blac stripes on the buttocks and tail and without the black stripes on the flanks.

DIFFERENCE BETWEEN ♂ AND ♀: The male is slightly heavier than the femal

HABITAT: Prefers dry open grass- and shrubveld and dry riverbeds. Important re quirements: sufficient plants to feed on, bushes that are not too high and dense an that block their movements and view. Avoids mountains, woodland and tall grass.

HABITS: Gregarious; usually forms small herds. There are mixed herds, bachelc herds and territorial males. Mixed herds split into nursing herds and new bachelc herds during the lambing season. Territories are maintained by showing-off display and marking with dung heaps, but are not occupied for the full year. Grazes in th early morning and late afternoon. "Pronks" when chased.

FOOD: Grass, sprouts and leaves of Karroo bushes and other herbs. Subsists withou water, but drinks when available, even stagnant water.

VOCALISATION: Low-pitched grumbling bellow. Whistling snort when upset

BREEDING: A single young is born anytime during the year, peaking in rain seasor after a gestation period of ± 6 months. ♀ has 1 (sometimes 2) pairs of groin mammae

AGE: ± 10 years.

KLIPSPRINGER   *Oreotragus oreotragus*

(KLIPSPRINGER)

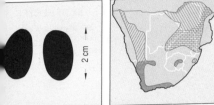

R.W.	Min: 4⅛″
	Max: 6¼″
S.C.I.	Min: 11″
	Max: 16⅞″
Mass:	♂ 9–12 kg
	♀ 11–16 kg
Shoulder height:	± 58 cm

IDENTIFICATION: Black speckles on brownish background provide good camouflage when in their rocky habitat. Large black "tearmarks" in the inner corners of the eyes.

DIFFERS FROM OTHER SPECIES: Common duiker: Slightly heavier, lacks the distinct black speckles on the coat and the black "tearmarks" in the corner of the eyes.

DIFFERENCE BETWEEN ♂ AND ♀: The female is heavier than the male and does not have horns.

HABITAT: Associated with rocky areas: mountains with rocks bordering ravines; ridges with rocks and juts, and rocky hills. Wanders over long distances. Independent of water.

HABITS: Mostly occurs in pairs, occasionally in family groups or single. Males establish their territories by forming dung heaps and scent-marking them with pre-orbital glands. Grazes in the early morning and late afternoon, even after dark, and rests in the shade in their rocky habitat. A very sure-footed rock climber. Closely confined to the rocky habitat. If disturbed while grazing on the surrounding flats, it immediately takes to rocky shelters.

FOOD: Mainly leaves, occasionally grass. Drinks water when available.

VOCALISATION: Alarm call: a loud, high-pitched explosion of air.

BREEDING: A single young is born anytime during the year after a gestation period of 7–7½ months. ♀ has 2 pairs of groin mammae.   **AGE:** ± 7 years.

DAMARA DIK-DIK *Madoqua kirkii*

(DAMARA-DIKDIK)

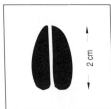

♂

♀

R.W.	Min: 2⅜″
	Max: 4″
S.C.I.	Min: 7″
	Max: 11⅞″
Mass:	4,3–5,5 kg
Shoulder	
height:	± 39 cm

IDENTIFICATION: A very small antelope. It has an elongated snout, white arou
the eyes. On top of the forehead is a tuft of long hair.

DIFFERS FROM OTHER SPECIES: Steenbok: Larger, of lighter colour and t
horns are vertical.

DIFFERENCE BETWEEN ♂ AND ♀: Only the male has horns.

HABITAT: Thickets and dense woodland on hard, stony ground with sufficie
shrubs and little or no grass. Also found against mountain slopes and in riverine fore
along which it can penetrate deep into deserts. Independent of water.

HABITS: Single, in pairs or in family groups of 3–6 during the dry season. The ma
probably establishes a territory in mating season. Grazes in the very early mornin
and late in the afternoons, even after dark. Rests during the hottest part of the day
thick cover. Uses the communal dung heap in a specific way: first smelling it, scratc
ing together a small heap on which it urinates before it defecates. The female do
the same, but does not scratch.

FOOD: Mainly leaves, occasionally green grass. Drinks when water is available.

VOCALISATION: An explosive whistling and a high trembling whistling soun

BREEDING: A single young is born from December–April after a gestation peric
of 5–6 months. ♀ have 2 pairs of groin mammae.

AGE: ± 9 years.

ORIBI *Ourebia ourebi*
(ORBIETJIE)

3,5 cm

SUBSPECIES

- *O.o. ourebi*
- *O.o. hastata*
- *O.o. rutila*

♂

♀

R.W.	Min: 5⅞"
	Max: 7½"
S.C.I.	Min: 13"
	Max: 18⅛"
Mass:	♂ 11–17 kg
	♀ 8–20 kg
Shoulder	♂ ± 58 cm
height:	♀ ± 59 cm

IDENTIFICATION: Small antelope with a rust-brown colour. The top part of the tail is black and there are black spots below the ears.

DIFFERS FROM OTHER SPECIES: Steenbok: Slightly smaller, without the long slender neck, black tail and black spots below the ears.

DIFFERENCE BETWEEN ♂ AND ♀: The female is heavier than the male and does not have horns.

HABITAT: Open grassveld or floodplains in well-watered areas, with or without scattered trees and shrubs. Found especially in areas with short grass and isolated patches of tall grass for shelter. Avoids large stretches of tall grass, woodland and dense bush.

HABITS: Mainly solitary, occasionally in pairs or small groups. The male is territorial and maintains this for the mating season through ostentation and by marking the grass with pre-orbital glands. Grazes when it is cool and rests in tall grass. Runs away prancing and leaping high if disturbed, but is very inquisitive and returns later. The male uses communal dung heaps, but this does not have any territorial function.

FOOD: Mainly grass, sometimes small branches. Does not drink water.

VOCALISATION: A snorting whistle as an alarm call.

BREEDING: A single young is born from October–December after a gestation period of ± 7 months. ♀ has 2 pairs of groin mammae. **AGE:** ± 13 years.

STEENBOK *Raphicerus campestris*

(STEENBOK)

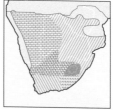

SUBSPECIES

	R.c. campestris
	R.c. fulvorubescens
	R.c. natalensis
	R.c. capricornis
	R.c. steinhardti

R.W.	Min: 4½"
	Max: 7½"
S.C.I.	Min: 11"
	Max: 18⅛"
Mass:	♂ 9–13 kg
	♀ 11–13 kg
Shoulder height:	± 52 cm

IDENTIFICATION: Small antelope with large ears. The insides of the ears ar
white with black stripes. There is a black stripe on top of the muzzle.

DIFFERS FROM OTHER SPECIES: Oribi: Larger, with a longer neck, a blac
tail and spots below the ears. Grysbok: White speckles on the body and longer hai

DIFFERENCE BETWEEN ♂ AND ♀: Only the male has horns.

HABITAT: Open grassveld with patches of tall grass or scattered bushes for shelte
Also in open woodland with bare patches and areas with fresh grass sprouting afte
a fire. Avoids mountainous areas and grassplains with short grass.

HABITS: Single or in pairs. Establishes territories that both the male and femal
defend by displays. There are preferential grazing and resting areas as well as latrine
close to the borders of such an area which are scent-marked with the pre-orbital, peda
and throat glands. Grazes during the cooler hours of the day and rests in tall grass c
beneath a bush when it is hot. Swift-footed, lies waiting until danger is almost upo
it before jumping up and running away.

FOOD: Leaves and grass, especially herbs. Seldom drinks water.

VOCALISATION: Bleats softly.

BREEDING: 1 (occasionally 2) young are born anytime during the year (possibl
peak November–December) after a gestation period of ± 6 months. ♀ has 2 pairs c
groin mammae.   **AGE:** ± 6 years.

80

CAPE GRYSBOK · *Raphicerus melanotis*

(KAAPSE GRYSBOK)

R.W.	Min: 3″
	Max: 4⅛″
S.C.I.	Min: 7″
	Max: 12⅛″
Mass:	9–12 kg
Shoulder height:	± 54 cm

IDENTIFICATION: A small antelope with large ears. The colour of the body is dark reddish-brown with white speckles. The face, legs and neck do not have speckles.

DIFFERS FROM OTHER SPECIES: Steenbok: Does not have white speckles on the body. Prefers more open areas. Sharpe's grysbok: Slightly smaller and of lighter colour.

DIFFERENCE BETWEEN ♂ AND ♀: Only the male has horns.

HABITAT: Prefers dense scrub along rivers, at the foot of mountains, ravines, broken country and even coastal forest. Occurs in arid areas containing succulents – sufficient shelter such as patches with dense shrubs are essential. Independent of water.

HABITS: Single or in pairs. Mainly nocturnal, but may graze late in the afternoons and rests in thick shelter during the hottest parts of the day. Always vigilant when moving about, lying down at the slightest sign of danger. Remains in this position until the last moment before leaping up and running away.

FOOD: Mainly grass, also leaves, young vine-shoots and wild fruit. Can go without water for a long period.

VOCALISATION: Unknown.

BREEDING: A single young is born from September–October after a gestation period of ± 6 months. ♀ has 2 pairs of groin mammae.

AGE: Unknown.

81

SHARPE'S GRYSBOK *Raphicerus sharpei*

(TROPIESE GRYSBOK)

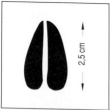

R.W.	Min: 1⅜"
	Max: 4⅛"
S.C.I.	Min: 5"
	Max: 8⅝"
Mass:	6,4–11,3 kg
Shoulder height:	45–50 cm

IDENTIFICATION: Small antelope. The colour of the body is light reddish-brown with white speckles. The head, neck and legs do not have speckles and there is a black stripe on the muzzle.

DIFFERS FROM OTHER SPECIES: Steenbok: Without white speckles. Prefer a more open habitat. Cape grysbok: Slightly larger and of darker colour.

DIFFERENCE BETWEEN ♂ AND ♀: Only the male has horns and the female is slightly larger than the male.

HABITAT: Areas with thick undergrowth of shrubs and/or grass of up to 50 cm height. Sometimes also found in rocky areas, but very fond of riverine flora and scrub surrounding koppies. Avoids areas with stretches of tall grass. Independent of water.

HABITS: Solitary or in pairs. Mainly nocturnal, but may be seen in the early mornings and especially late afternoons. Active for longer periods on cool, overcast days. Rests during the hottest hours of the day beneath a bush or other thick cover. Vigilant and timid; runs away with the body close to the ground.

FOOD: Mainly leaves, also grass, young sprouts, roots and wild fruit.

VOCALISATION: Unknown.

BREEDING: A single young is born anytime during the year after a gestation period of ± 7 months. ♀ has 2 pairs of groin mammae.

AGE: Unknown.

82

SUNI (Livingstone's antelope)   *Neotragus moschatus*
(SOENIE)

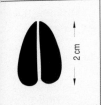

SUBSPECIES

N.m. livingstonianus

N.m. zuluensis

R.W.	Min: 3"
	Max: 5¼"
S.C.I.	Min: 9"
	Max: 13⅝"
Mass:	♂ 4,5–5,2 kg
	♀ 5,1–6,8 kg
Shoulder height:	± 35 cm

IDENTIFICATION: One of the smallest antelope. The tail is long, dark and has a white edge. The upper lip protrudes over the lower lip.

DIFFERS FROM OTHER SPECIES: Red duiker: Larger and more reddish. The horns are closer together and the tail is shorter and not as dark.

DIFFERENCE BETWEEN ♂ AND ♀: Female has no horns; heavier than male.

HABITAT: Prefers dry savannah with sufficient undergrowth and scrub for cover, as well as riverine forest and dry bush along tributaries. Also found in deciduous woodland with thick undergrowth. Independent of water.

HABITS: Solitary, pairs or family groups. Diurnal: grazes in the early mornings and late afternoons – for longer periods in cooler weather. Rests during the hottest part of the day. Shy and is seldom seen. When disturbed it stands dead still for a while before it runs off making a "chee-chee" sound. Use communal dung heaps and have small home ranges, may be territorial. Uses footpaths in dense bush and is easily caught in traps.

FOOD: Leaves and wild fruit. Does not drink water.

VOCALISATION: Snorts and makes a high pitched "chee-chee" whistling sound. (Softer than that of the red duiker.)

BREEDING: A single young is born from August–February after a gestation period of ± 4 months. ♀ has 2 pairs of groin mammae.

AGE: Unknown.

IMPALA *Aepyceros melampus*
(ROOIBOK)

5-6 cm

SUBSPECIES

A.m. melampus:
Reddish brown, no black blaze on face

A.m. petersi:
Dull brown, purple sheen, black blaze and stripes at eyes (swartneusrooibok)

Black-faced impala   Impala

R.W.	Min: 23⅝"	
	Max: 31⅞"	
S.C.I.	Min: 54"	
	Max: 67⅝"	
Mass:	♂	47–82 kg
	♀	32–52 kg
Shoulder	♂	± 90 cm
height:	♀	± 86 cm

IDENTIFICATION: Athletically-built medium-sized antelope. There are charac
teristic black bands on the tail and buttocks. Patches of black hair occur above ankles
DIFFERS FROM OTHER SPECIES: Reedbuck: Greyish-brown with a yellov
sheen. Puku: Golden-brown. Both do not have the black bands on the buttocks and tai.
DIFFERENCE BETWEEN ♂ AND ♀: The female is smaller and has no horns .
HABITAT: Open woodland with sufficient water – especially thorn- and mopaniveld
also found in more dense woodland such as that along rivers (especially the black-face
impala); and on the edge of woodland and grassveld or floodplains. Dependent on wate
HABITS: Gregarious; usually forms herds of 6–20 and even more than 100 in winte
Territorial males (only in mating season), bachelor herds and breeding herds can be dis
tinguished. During the rest of the year territorial males join breeding or bachelor herds
Adult males establish territories during the mating season; they use communal dung
heaps and scent-mark the grass and bushes with the pre-orbital glands. Mainly diurna
and rests in shade during the hottest part of the day.
FOOD: Leaves and grass. Drinks water daily when available.
VOCALISATION: An alarm snort. Adult males make a roaring-rattling sound and
snort, especially during the mating season.
BREEDING: A single young is born from September–January after a gestation
period of ± 6 months. ♀ has 2 pairs of groin mammae.   **AGE:** ± 12 years.

GREY RHEBOK *Pelea capreolus*
(VAALRIBBOK)

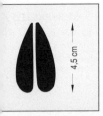

4,5 cm

SUBSPECIES
None.

♂

♀

R.W.	Min: 7⅞"
	Max: 11½"
S.C.I.	Min: 18"
	Max: 26⅜"
Mass:	18–23 kg
Shoulder height:	± 74 cm

IDENTIFICATION: Long, thin neck with very long pointed upright ears. The horns are straight and stand upright.

DIFFERS FROM OTHER SPECIES: Mountain reedbuck: Horns bent forward and black spots below the ears. The neck is shorter and thicker and the ears are rounded.

DIFFERENCE BETWEEN ♂ AND ♀: Male has horns; heavier than female.

HABITAT: Rocky mountains, mountain slopes and plateaus with sufficient grass and a few shrubs and trees. Utilizes a more exposed habitat than the mountain reedbuck – grass slopes of the Drakensberg between 1 400 m and 2 500 m above sea level. Independent of water.

HABITS: Forms herds of up to 12 animals. There are solitary males and family groups (with a territorial male) but no bachelor herds. When a young male leaves the group, he remains solitary until he is old enough to establish his own territory. A part of the family group's home range is the territorial male's territory. He advertises this with certain movements and ostentations. The rhebok grazes with short resting periods and rests for 3 hours during the hottest part of the day.

FOOD: Grass.

VOCALISATION: Snorts and hisses and an alarm cough.

BREEDING: A single young is born from December–January after a gestation period of ± 8 months. ♀ has 2 pairs of groin mammae.   **AGE:** ± 9 years.

85

ROAN ANTELOPE (Roan) *Hippotragus equinus*

(BASTERGEMSBOK)

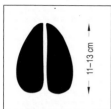

SUBSPECIES

H.e. equinus

H.e. cottoni

Large overlapping in North-west Zimbabwe.

R.W.	Min:	27″
	Max:	39″
S.C.I.	Min:	68″
	Max:	81⅝″
Mass:	230–272 kg	
Shoulder height:	± 143 cm	

IDENTIFICATION: Very large antelope. Both sexes have scimitar-like horns and very long ears. The face seems to have a black mask with white patches in front of the eyes and around the mouth.

DIFFERENCE BETWEEN ♂ AND ♀: The male is slightly larger than the female and its horns are thicker.

HABITAT: Very specific requirements: open savannah with large stretches of medium to tall grass and sufficient water. Very sensitive to any change in habitat such as bush encroachment and overutilisation of grass. Tolerates scattered short shrubs. Avoids thickets, areas with short grass and woodland with roof of foliage.

HABITS: Bachelor herds, solitary males and breeding herds exist (5–25 animals/herd). A breeding herd with a dominant male and a female as leader will leave their home range only if food and water become scarce. The male shows territorial behaviour, but merely defends his females (300–500 m around the herd) and not a specific area. When a young male becomes an adult (5–6 years) it leaves the bachelor herd and goes solitary. Grazes in the early mornings and late afternoons.

FOOD: Grass (from 2–8 cm) and sometimes also leaves.

VOCALISATION: Something between a snort and a hissing sound.

BREEDING: A single young is born anytime during the year after a gestation period of 9–9½ months. ♀ has 2 pairs of groin mammae. **AGE:** ± 19 years.

86

ABLE ANTELOPE (Sable) *Hippotragus niger*
(/ARTWITPENS)

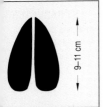

SUBSPECIES

Only one subspecies occurs in the region.

▨ *H.n. niger*

♀   ♂

R.W.	Min: 41⅞"
	Max: 60¾"
S.C.I.	Min: 100"
	Max: 124⅝"
Mass:	180–250 kg
Shoulder height:	± 140 cm

IDENTIFICATION: These large antelope are dark brown to black and have white bellies. The face is white with dark stripes and both sexes have scimitar-like horns.

DIFFERENCE BETWEEN ♂ AND ♀: The female is usually browner and slightly smaller than the male and the horns are thinner and shorter.

HABITAT: Shelter and water are important requirements – seldom found further than 3 km from water. Prefers open woodland or woodland near vleis or grassveld with medium to tall grass; even in dense woodland on well-drained soil (where roan antelopes do not occur). Avoids dense savannah and areas with short grass.

HABITS: Territorial males, nursing herds and bachelor herds exist (10–30 animals/herd). A territorial male defends his area with intimidating displays. Nursing herds with one or more dominant females as leaders move through the territories of males. Young males (3 years) join bachelor herds and remain there until they are 5–6 years old. Grazes early in the mornings and late afternoons.

FOOD: Mainly grass, sometimes leaves at the end of a dry season. Drinks water at least once a day, usually between 10:00 and 16:00.

VOCALISATION: Snorts, bellows and sneezes.

BREEDING: A single young is born from January–March after a gestation period ± 8 months. ♀ has 2 pairs of groin mammae.   **AGE:** ± 17 years.

GEMSBOK *Oryx gazella*
(GEMSBOK)

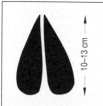

SUBSPECIES

Only one subspecies occurs in the region.

▦ *O.g. gazella*

R.W.	Min: 40″
	Max: 49¼″
S.C.I.	Min: 88″
	Max: 108½″
Mass:	♂ ± 240 kg
	♀ ± 210 kg
Shoulder height:	± 120 cm

IDENTIFICATION: Large antelope, with both sexes having long, straight hor▪ The face is black with white marks and the tail is long and black.

DIFFERENCE BETWEEN ♂ AND ♀: The male is slightly heavier than the fema and the horns are thicker and usually shorter.

HABITAT: Associated with open, dry landscape. Prefers open grassveld in semid sert areas and open dry savannah. May even penetrate open woodland in search new grazing areas. In the Kalahari it prefers the sand dune midland with scatter plant cover and short one-year grass.

HABITS: There are nursing and mixed herds, territorial and other solitary males (. 12 animals/herd). Territorial males are very tolerant of other males and often accor pany mixed herds. They mark their territories by horning and scratching the grou and defecating in a squatting position so that the dung lies in a heap to retain the sm longer.

FOOD: Grass, sometimes also tsammas, succulent rhizomes and tubers. Subsis without water for a long time, but drinks if available. Digs for water in sand at time

VOCALISATION: Bellows like cattle.

BREEDING: A single young is born anytime during the year after a gestation peri of ± 9 months. ♀ has 2 pairs groin mammae.

AGE: ± 19 years.

JFFALO *Cyncerus caffer*

(FFEL)

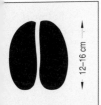

SUBSPECIES

Only one subspecies occurs in the region.

▨ *S.c. caffer*

R.W.	Min:	45″
	Max:	64″
S.C.I.	Min:	100″
	Max:	139⅛″
Mass:	♂	750–820 kg
	♀	680–750 kg
Shoulder	♂	± 170 cm
height:	♀	± 140 cm

ENTIFICATION: Large, cattle-like animals. Greyish-black, assumes the colour the soil at times when it wallows in the mud. Both sexes have horns.

IFFERENCE BETWEEN ♂ AND ♀: The male is usually darker and heavier than e female and has larger horns.

ABITAT: Enough edible grass, shade and water are important requirements. Pref-ential grass occurs in mopani and thornveld, as well as in other types of woodland d open vleis. Avoids floodplains or grassveld that is far from the shade of trees.

ABITS: Forms herds which can number a few thousand. Split into smaller herds summer, moving apart in search of good grazing, but when it becomes drier return areas with permanent water. Mixed and bachelor herds as well as solitary males n be distinguished. There is a definite hierarchy between males that is maintained threatening behaviour. Dangerous animals to hunt: A wounded buffalo may circle ck, wait for the hunter along its track and attack him. Grazes when it is cool and sts in the shade during the hottest part of the day.

OOD: Grass, drinks water regularly/twice a day (early morning and late afternoon).

OCALISATION: Bellows like cattle or grunts when in a fight.

REEDING: A single young is born in summer after a gestation period of ± 11 onths. ♀ has 2 pairs of groin mammae.

GE: ± 23 years.

KUDU *Tragelaphus strepsiceros*
(KOEDOE)

8–9,5 cm

R.W.	Min: 53⅞"
	Max: 69¼"
S.C.I.	Min: 121"
	Max: 150½"
Mass:	♂ 190–270 kg
	♀ 120–210 kg
Shoulder	♂ ± 150 cm
height:	♀ ± 135 cm

IDENTIFICATION: Large, elegant antelope with impressive horns and white stripes on the flanks. The female has prominent ears. The male becomes dark against the neck when the hair falls out.

DIFFERENCE BETWEEN ♂ AND ♀: Female: Smaller than male, no horns.

HABITAT: A savannah species: Occurs even in dry semidesert areas that have sufficient food and shrubs for shelter. Prefers open woodland (especially thornveld) and rocky terrain with water nearby. Prefers wooded areas along streams in dry areas

HABITS: Form herds of 4–12 animals, consisting of females and their young males. In the mating season an adult male is accompanied by a few females and young. Out of season the males go solitary or form bachelor herds of up to 6 animals. Grazes in the early mornings and late afternoons; rests in the shade during the hotter part of the day. Very timid and takes off to shelter at the slightest sign of danger. When it runs away its tail is turned upwards so that the white underparts show – a sign of alarm and direction.

FOOD: Leaves, sometimes sprouts, pods (especially thorn trees) and even fresh grass

VOCALISATION: A very loud hoarse cough.

BREEDING: A single young is born anytime during the year with a peak in late summer after a gestation period of ± 7 months. ♀ has 2 pairs of groin mammae.

AGE: ± 14 years.

TATUNGA *Tragelaphus spekei*
(ATERKOEDOE)

7–8,5 cm

♂   ♀

SUBSPECIES

Only one subspecies
occurs in the region.

▨   *T.s. selousi*

R.W.	Min: 27⅛″
	Max: 32½″
S.C.I.	Min: 60″
	Max: 81⅝″
Mass:	♂ ± 114 kg
	♀ ± 55 kg
Shoulder	♂ ± 114 cm
height:	♀ ± 90 cm

IDENTIFICATION: A large semi-aquatic antelope. Resembles a nyala. The hooves are long and splayed. The male has a chevron mark between its eyes.

DIFFERS FROM OTHER SPECIES: Bushbuck (Chobe): Smaller, the male has smaller horns, more reddish and does not live in the swamps.

DIFFERENCE BETWEEN ♂ AND ♀: Only the male has horns and the female usually is of lighter colour and is much smaller than the male.

HABITAT: Lives mostly in the water even up to 1 m deep. Prefers papyrus and common reedbeds in swamps or flooded areas in Okavango and Chobe rivers. Grazes in shallow water on water-grass but avoids open floodplains.

HABITS: Lives in small herds with a male, females and young of up to 6 animals and when they graze they spread out. Single animals also occur. Grazes throughout the day but rests during the hottest part of the day on platforms of broken-down reeds and other debris in the papyrus. Moves out at night to the surrounding woodland or islands and returns before dawn. Very good swimmers.

FOOD: Water-grass, papyrus, reed shoots and fresh leaves.

VOCALISATION: Drawn out alarm bark (similar to bushbuck) which is repeated.

BREEDING: A single young is born anytime during the year (peaks in June–July). Has 2 pairs of groin mammae.

AGE: ± 19 years.

91

NYALA *Tragelaphus angasii*

(NJALA)

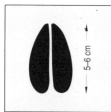

SUBSPECIES

None.

R.W.	Min: 27″
	Max: 32¾″
S.C.I.	Min: 63″
	Max: 82½″
Mass:	♂ 92–126 kg
	♀ 55–68 kg
Shoulder	♂ ± 112 cm
height:	♀ ± 97 cm

IDENTIFICATION: Elegant, slender antelope. The male has a white chevron ma[r]
between the eyes, white-tipped mane and yellow "socks".

DIFFERS FROM OTHER SPECIES: Bushbuck ♀: Smaller and browner tha[n]
nyala ♀, usually without stripes.

DIFFERENCE BETWEEN ♂ **AND** ♀: Only the male has horns. The female [is]
lighter in colour and much smaller.

HABITAT: Associated with thickets in dry woodland. This includes dense wood[-]
land, riverine forests, island bush in floodplains and other thickets. Surroundin[g]
floodplains and grassplains are visited when grass sprouts. Dependent on water.

HABITS: Forms temporary herds of 3–30 animals with home ranges overlappin[g].
Solitary young ones, females and males, young male herds, adult male herds, femal[e]
herds, family herds and mixed herds can be distinguished. Family herds are the mo[st]
stable of all. The male horns the ground or lifts its mane when another male is nearb[y].
Grazes when it is cool, even at night, and rests during the hottest part of the day.

FOOD: Leaves, branches, fruit and flowers. Drinks water daily when available.

VOCALISATION: The female makes a "click" sound, young ones bleat. A dee[p]
bark as an alarm call.

BREEDING: A single young is born anytime during the year (peaks in Aug–Dec[).]
gestation period ± 7 months. ♀ has 2 pairs of groin mammae. **AGE:** ± 13 years[.]

92

BUSHBUCK *Tragelaphus scriptus*
(BOSBOK)

Chobe bushbuck

Limpopo bushbuck

R.W.	Min: 14″
	Max: 19⅝″
S.C.I.	Min: 31″
	Max: 55⅛″
Mass:	♂ 40–77 kg
	♀ 30–36 kg
Shoulder	♂ ± 80 cm
height:	♀ ± 70 cm

IDENTIFICATION: Timid medium-sized antelope. White spots on the buttocks, against the legs, at the base of the neck and against the throat.

DIFFERS FROM OTHER SPECIES: Nyala ♀: Larger, more yellow with white stripes. Situtunga: Larger than Chobe bushbuck, not as reddish-brown and lives in swamps.

DIFFERENCE BETWEEN ♂ AND ♀: Only the male has horns, it is larger and darker than those of the female.

HABITAT: Prefers riverine forests or other types of dense thickets near perennial water. May move in summer to other thickets near temporary water sources, returning when it becomes dry. Dependent on water and sufficient shelter.

HABITS: Usually solitary, now and then seen in pairs, small groups of females, females with their young or small bachelor herds. Stays in riverine forest during the winter when it has a smaller home range than in the wet season. Usually grazes at night or early mornings and late afternoons and rests during the day in thickets. Has keen senses. The male is very brave and will even attack when wounded.

FOOD: Mainly leaves. Also grass, branches, flowers and fruit.

VOCALISATION: Grumbles and a loud hoarse bark as an alarm call.

BREEDING: A single young is born anytime during the year after a gestation period of ± 6 months. ♀ has 2 pairs of groin mammae   **AGE:** ± 11 years.

93

ELAND *Taurotragus oryx*

(ELAND)

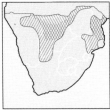

SUBSPECIES

▨ *T.o. oryx:* Without white side stripes

▨ *T.o. livingstonii:* 6–7 white side stripes

▨ Large area of intergradation: 1–3 white side stripes

R.W.	Min: 35″
	Max: 44¼″
S.C.I.	Min: 79″
	Max: 115⅞″
Mass:	♂ ± 700 kg
	♀ ± 460 kg
Shoulder	♂ ± 170 cm
height:	♀ ± 150 cm

IDENTIFICATION: The region's largest antelope. Resembles a Brahman with it large hump and dewlap. Both sexes have horns. As the male ages it becomes darke on the neck.

DIFFERENCE BETWEEN ♂ AND ♀: The male is larger and much heavier tha the female and its horns are thicker and heavier.

HABITAT: Very adaptable: found from semidesert shrubveld to different types c woodland and moist mountain grassland (Mozambique). Trees and shrubs are im portant. Avoids vast open grassplains. Independent of water.

HABITS: Usually forms small herds, but large herds of hundreds have been seer The hierarchy in the herds is based on age and size. In the calving season, nursir herds and bachelor herds can be distinguished. At a later stage young animals an males join the nursing herds and form breeding herds. Breeding herds are placi while serious fights occur in bachelor herds. During the winter males and female leave the nursing herds and form mixed or bachelor herds. Also grazes at night. characteristic clicking sound can be heard when they walk.

FOOD: Mainly leaves, sometimes grass. Drinks water regularly when available.

VOCALISATION: Females "moo", calves bleat, adults bellow, bark and grumble

BREEDING: A single young is born anytime during the year (peaks in Aug–Oct gestation period ± 9 months. ♀ has 2 pairs of groin mammae.　**AGE:** ± 12 year

EEDBUCK (Southern reedbuck) *Redunca arundinum*
.TBOK)

5,5 cm

SUBSPECIES

Only one subspecies occurs in the region.

▦ *R.a. arundinum*

R.W.	Min: 14″
	Max: 18⅜″
S.C.I.	Min: 34″
	Max: 53⅜″
Mass:	♂ ± 80 kg
	♀ ± 70 kg
Shoulder	♂ ± 90 cm
height:	♀ ± 80 cm

ENTIFICATION: Medium-sized antelope with yellowish grey-brown colour d sometimes black spots below the ears. The front of the forelegs is dark brown.

IFFERS FROM OTHER SPECIES: Mountain reedbuck: Smaller, greyish and efers mountainous habitat. Impala: Redder, three black stripes: two on the buttocks d one on the tail.

IFFERENCE BETWEEN ♂ AND ♀: Only the male has horns and is larger.

ABITAT: Always in or near vleis or reed beds with open water. Also floodplains d other grassplains (with tall grass) along rivers or marshes with perennial water. voids thickets and woodland. Dependent on water and reeds for shelter.

ABITS: Usually lives in pairs, occupying a territory. Although larger groups are und, it is not gregarious. Territorial male defends his area with threatening dis- ays. He defecates and urinates in front of his challenger, standing on stiff legs th the head held up high. Younger male shows his submission to territorial male bowing his head. If grazing is in a good condition it becomes nocturnal; and dur- g the dry season more diurnal.

OOD: Mainly grass. Drinks water regularly, even more than once a day on warm days.

OCALISATION: A high-pitched whistle through the nostrils as an alarm call.

REEDING: A single young is born anytime during the year after a gestation period 7–8 months. ♀ has 2 pairs of groin mammae.   **AGE:** ± 9 years.

95

MOUNTAIN REEDBUCK *Redunca fulvorufula*

(ROOIRIBBOK)

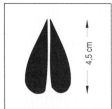

4,5 cm

SUBSPECIES

Only one subspecies occurs in the region.

R.f. fulvorufula

R.W.	Min: 6⅞"
	Max: 11½"
S.C.I.	Min: 20"
	Max: 30⅝"
Mass:	♂ 24–36 kg
	♀ 15–34 kg
Shoulder	♂ ± 75 cm
height:	♀ ± 73 cm

IDENTIFICATION: Medium-sized antelope with black spots below the ears. T colour of the body is greyish with a red sheen and the neck is brown. The points the ears are rounded.

DIFFERS FROM OTHER SPECIES: Grey rhebok: The neck is also grey and longer and thinner. Horns are straight and the ears are more upright and pointed. Ree buck: Larger, of a brighter yellow, black stripes on the forelegs and prefers marshy are

DIFFERENCE BETWEEN ♂ AND ♀: Female: Smaller than male, no horns.

HABITAT: Associated with mountainous areas. Dry rocky slopes of mountains a hills with sufficient grass and shelter such as scattered trees and shrubs. Usua avoids open plateaus and peaks. Dependent on water.

HABITS: Usually forms herds of 3–6 (sometimes up to 30). Territorial males, oth solitary males, nursing herds and bachelor herds can be distinguished. Nursing her are unstable and move over the territories of several males. Grazes when it is co even at night and rests during the hottest part of the day in the shade. When alarm it flees downhill, while grey rhebok flees to higher areas.

FOOD: Mainly grass. Drinks water regularly, especially in dry, warm weather.

BREEDING: A single young is born anytime during the year (peaks in Decembe January) after a gestation period of ± 8 months. ♀ has 2 pairs of groin mammae.

VOCALISATION: A shrill whistle similar to that of the reedbuck.   **AGE:** ± 11 yea

WATERBUCK *Kobus ellipsiprymnus*
(WATERBOK)

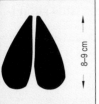

8–9 cm

R.W.	Min: 28″
	Max: 39¼″
S.C.I.	Min: 70″
	Max: 91⅝″
Mass:	♂ 250–270 kg
	♀ 205–250 kg
Shoulder ♂	± 170 cm
height: ♀	± 130 cm

IDENTIFICATION: Large greyish-brown antelope with white circle around the tail. The hair is coarse, shaggy and long.

DIFFERENCE BETWEEN ♂ AND ♀: The female is smaller than the male and does not have horns.

HABITAT: A savannah species: never far away from water, but normally avoids riverine forests. Found in woodland along rivers, dry floodplains and vleis or in reed beds along marshes. These areas usually have good quality grass for grazing. Very dependent on water.

HABITS: Usually forms herds of 6–12 (even up to 30). There are territorial males, nursing herds and bachelor herds. Herds become larger in summer but divide in winter. Young males become fully grown at about 5–6 years and then try to establish territory. Territories are defended by threatening displays. A subordinate lowers his head as a sign of submission. Serious fights are very common. If a nursing herd passes across a male's territory, the male will try to round up the females.

FOOD: Mainly grass, sometimes leaves and fruit. Drinks water regularly.

VOCALISATION: Snorts and a soft "moo" sound when the female calls her calf.

BREEDING: 1 (occasionally 2) young are born anytime during the year after a gestation period of ± 9 months. ♀ has 2 pairs of groin mammae.

AGE: ± 14 years.

RED LECHWE *Kobus leche*

(BASTERWATERBOK)

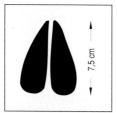

SUBSPECIES

Only one subspecies occurs in the region.

 K.l. leche

R.W.	Min: 26″
	Max: 35″
S.C.I.	Min: 58″
	Max: 73⅝″
Mass:	♂ 100–130 kg
	♀ 61–97 kg
Shoulder	♂ ± 104 cm
height:	♀ ± 97 cm

IDENTIFICATION: Medium-sized antelope with characteristic dark markings on the forelegs. The shoulders are lower than the croup, body slants forward.
DIFFERS FROM OTHER SPECIES: Puku: Smaller, more gold-brown, less white on the belly and without the dark markings on the forelegs.
DIFFERENCE BETWEEN ♂ AND ♀: The female is smaller and has no horns.
HABITAT: Always in or near water. On shallow-flooded floodplains (up to 50 c deep) along swamps and rivers, or in areas between papyrus or reed beds and the sta of dry land. Uses areas with shallower water than sitatunga.
HABITS: Usually form herds of 10–30. Larger aggregations sometimes occur. Bach lor herds, nursing herds and solitary adult males can be distinguished. During the mati season a few males establish small territories which they share with some nursing her so as to establish a breeding area. Other males are allowed if they are not interested the male's females, or else driven out by threatening displays. Usually grazes in the ear mornings and late afternoons and rests during the heat of day on dry ground.
FOOD: Water-grass and other grass. Drinks water regularly (up to 3 times a day)
VOCALISATION: A low whistle and a whinnying-grunt as an alarm call.
BREEDING: A single young is born anytime during the year (peaks in Octobe December) after a gestation period of 7–8 months. ♀ has 2 pairs of groin mamma
AGE: Unknown.

PUKU *Kobus vardonii*
(POEKOE)

6-7 cm

♂

♀

R.W.	Min:	16⅞″
	Max:	22⅛″
S.C.I.	Min:	46″
	Max:	58″
Mass:	♂	68–91 kg
	♀	48–80 kg
Shoulder	♂	± 81 cm
height:	♀	± 78 cm

IDENTIFICATION: Medium-sized antelope with a golden-brown colour virtually all over the body; the belly, throat and areas around the mouth are whitish.

DIFFERS FROM OTHER SPECIES: Red lechwe: Larger, reddish-brown, more white on the belly. Black markings against the forelegs. Impala: A brighter red, 3 black stripes on the buttocks and tail.

DIFFERENCE BETWEEN ♂ AND ♀: The female is smaller and has no horns.

HABITAT: A specialized habitat: the grass areas directly along or around water. Utilizes the narrow stretches of grassplains between marsh or floodplains and the woodland on surrounding higher ground. Dependent on water.

HABITS: Forms herds with loose association of 2–28. Territorial males, female herds and bachelor herds can be distinguished. Territories are not defended all the time, and sexually inactive males are allowed. If a female herd passes through a male's territory, he will try to round them up. Bachelor herds' home ranges are separate from those of the females and territorial males. Grazes in the early mornings, late afternoons until after sunset. Often seen together with impala.

FOOD: Mainly grass.

VOCALISATION: An alarm whistle – repeated up to 5 times.

BREEDING: A single young is born anytime during the year (peaks in May–Sept), gestation period ± 8 months. ♀ has 2 pairs of groin mammae.   **AGE:** Unknown.

99

PANGOLIN (Scaly ant-eater) *Manis temminckii*
(IETERMAGOG)

7 cm

SUBSPECIES
None.

Mass: 4,5–14,5 kg

Length: ± 81 cm

IDENTIFICATION: Very hard, strong imbricated scales all over the body, except the underparts and the sides of the face which are bare. Well-developed claws on the forepaws.

DIFFERENCE BETWEEN ♂ AND ♀: None.

HABITAT: Occurs in a variety of habitat types: from bushy veld in the arid parts (250 mm/annum) to different types of woodlands in humid savannah areas. Occurs also on rocky hills, sandveld and floodplain grassveld. Ants and termites (on which it feeds) and shelter (such as holes or piles of vegetable debris to rest in) are important requirements.

HABITS: Mainly nocturnal and solitary. Walks on its hindlegs, balancing so that the tail and forelegs touch the ground only now and then. Very shy and stands dead still if disturbed. If followed stands stretched on its hindlegs, supported with the tail, to watch the vicinity. Rolls into a tight ball when in danger. Rests during the day in old antbear or springhare holes and/or rock crevices.

FOOD: Mainly ants, sometimes termites. Has a very long sticky tongue and no teeth.

VOCALISATION: Unknown.

BREEDING: A single young is born from May–July after a gestation period of ± 4 months. ♀ has 1 pair of breast mammae.

AGE: ± 12 years.

100

APE HARE *Lepus capensis*
(AKHAAS)

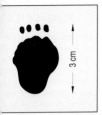

3 cm

SUBSPECIES

16 Subspecies: Very difficult to distinguish. Examples from desert and semi-desert usually smaller and paler.

Mass: ♂ 1,4–1,8 kg
         ♀ 1,5–2,3 kg

Length: ± 47 cm

ENTIFICATION: The smallest of the two hares. Colour varies a lot but the tail usually dull-black on top and white underneath.

FFERS FROM OTHER SPECIES: Scrub hare: Larger and usually has a white ch on the forehead. Prefers a denser environment.

FFERENCE BETWEEN ♂ **AND** ♀: The male is slightly smaller than the female.

ABITAT: Prefers open dry areas, grassplains in the vicinity of pans and other ssy areas. Edible grass and shelter to rest in such as low shrubs or tufts of grass e essential. Independent of water.

ABITS: Although mainly nocturnal, also seen on cool, overcast days. Less active cold weather. Does not appear when it rains. Rests during the day lying beneath hrub or tuft of grass with the ears flat, dependent on its camouflage. Jumps into bear or springhare holes when fleeing – something a scrub hare does not do. ually solitary. In mating season, males may fight over a female.

OOD: Only grass, especially short grass. Gets enough moisture from food and dew.

OCALISATION: Normally silent. Snorts or screams when handled.

REEDING: 1–3 young are born anytime during the year (peaks in summer) after estation period of ± 6 weeks.

;E: ± 5 years.

SCRUB HARE *Lepus saxatilis*

(KOLHAAS)

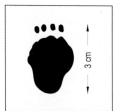

SUBSPECIES

6 Subspecies occur in the south of its distribution are and are not easily identifie Examples in South Wester Cape are larger and becom smaller with smaller ears towards the north-west.

Mass: ♂ 1,4–3,8 kg
♀ 1,6–4,5 kg

Length: ± 55 cm

IDENTIFICATION: Largest of the two hares. Dull yellow with greyish speck (salt-and-pepper effect). Nape brown to orange. White patch on forehead.

DIFFERS FROM OTHER SPECIES: Cape hare: Smaller, does not occur in scr – prefers open dry grassveld.

DIFFERENCE BETWEEN ♂ AND ♀: The male is slightly smaller than the fema

HABITAT: A savannah species: scrub areas with patches of grass. Avoids dense bu or open grassplains. Grazes at night in open areas. Sufficient edible grass and de shrub for shelter are important requirements. Independent of water.

HABITS: Mainly nocturnal, but may graze in the mornings on cool, overcast da Sensitive to cold weather: scarce on cold nights and if it rains it remains in its shelt Rests during the day beneath a shrub with some grass close by. Lies down with ears flat and the head placed close to the body and leaps up when danger is very ne Runs with a swerving and turning movement. Usually solitary but in mating seas one or more males keep close to a female.

FOOD: Grass and rhizomes. Prefers green grass. Gets enough moisture from foo

VOCALISATION: Normaly silent. A loud scream when handled.

BREEDING: 1–3 young are born anytime during the year (may peak in Septe ber–February) after a gestation period of ± 5 weeks.

AGE: ± 7 years.

GROUND SQUIRREL   *Xerus inauris*
(WAAIERSTERT-GRONDEEKHORING)

SUBSPECIES
None.

Mass: ♂ 511–1022 g
        ♀ 511–795 g

Length: ± 45 cm

IDENTIFICATION: Characteristic white stripes on its sides, and a white belly. The "fan" tail is bushy and white and brown and is sometimes spread over the back for shade.

DIFFERS FROM OTHER SPECIES: Mountain ground squirrel: Looks the same but its burrows are mostly on rocky hills or banks of rocks which are avoided by ground squirrel.

DIFFERENCE BETWEEN ♂ AND ♀: The male is slightly heavier than the female.

HABITAT: Only found in dry areas. Prefers open country with scattered bushes on hard or calcareous soil (avoids loose sandy soil). Also found along dry streams on dry floodplains or in open karrooveld. Independent of water.

HABITS: Gregarious: forms colonies of up to 30, and lives in a burrow, which it digs with different entrances, rooms and corridors. Rooms are layered with grass to rest on. The colonies consist of females and their young. Males move between groups and stay only temporarily. They share the burrows sometimes with suricates and/or yellow mongoose. Diurnal: only appears after sunrise and returns before sunset. They often groom themselves and one another.

FOOD: Grass, leaves, tubers, seeds, roots, stems and sometimes insects.

VOCALISATION: High-pitched whistle or scream as alarm. Aggressive grumble.

BREEDING: 1–3 young are born anytime during the year after a gestation period of 6–7 weeks. ♀ has 2 pairs of groin mammae.   **AGE:** ± 15 years.

TREE SQUIRREL *Paraxerus cepapi*

(BOOMEEKHORING)

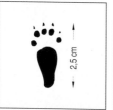

SUBSPECIES

	P.c. cepapi
	P.c. carpi
	P.c. cepapoides
	P.c. chobiensis
	P.c. phalaena
	P.c. sindi
	P.c. maunensis
	P.c. kalaharicus
	P.c. tsumebensis

In arid areas their colour is lighter than in moist areas.

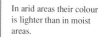

Mass:	♂	76–240 g
	♀	108–265 g
Length:	♀	± 35 cm

IDENTIFICATION: Well-known savannah squirrel. Greyish-brown speckled with a long bushy tail and yellow on the flanks.

DIFFERS FROM OTHER SPECIES: Red squirrel: Tail, legs and belly are more yellow or reddish than the body. Sun squirrel: Larger, the full length of the tail is ringed with a lighter colour.

DIFFERENCE BETWEEN ♂ AND ♀: None.

HABITAT: In most types of savannah, especially mopani and thornveld and mixed savannah. As it requires holes in tree trunks to rest or make a nest in, old mopani and thorn trees are popular. Independent of water.

HABITS: Usually solitary. In Transvaal they live in groups of a few adults and young ones defining an area and marking it with scent. They groom and scent-mark one another and chase away strangers. If a predator is seen, it takes off to a safe place and teases the predator with chattering and flicking of tail. Grazes on the ground and is always alert, takes off to nest or nearest tree at the slightest disturbance – always keeping the tree between itself and the threat.

FOOD: Leaves, seeds, fruit, flowers, bark, thorntree gum, lichen and insects.

VOCALISATION: Bird-like "cheek-chik-chik-chik" sounds and chattering.

BREEDING: 1–3 young are born anytime during the year (peaks in October–April) Gestation period ± 8 weeks. ♀ has 3 pairs of mammae.   **AGE:** ± 8 years.

SPRINGHARE *Pedetes capensis*
(SPRINGHAAS)

SUBSPECIES

Only one subspecies occurs in the region.

▨ *P.c. capensis*

Mass: 2,5–3,8 kg

Length: ± 80 cm

IDENTIFICATION: Resembles a kangaroo with the long hindlegs for leaping, and short forelegs. The tail ends in a characteristic black broad tip.

DIFFERENCE BETWEEN ♂ AND ♀: None.

HABITAT: Compacted sandy soil for digging holes. Areas with precipitations of sandy silt along rivers is an important requirement. Also found in sandy country or sandy shrubby veld. Avoids hard clay soil. Holes are usually on higher ground. Independent of water.

HABITS: Nocturnal, only appears when it is quite dark. They are keen excavators; loosening the soil with the forelegs, working it out with the hindlegs. The burrows in which they live slope down for a few metres and at a depth of about 1 m become level again. On the farthest side an escape hole is dug. Burrows may have corridors and more than one entrance and emergency exit. Only one springhare lives in a hole. There will be tracks on the heap of soil outside the hole if it is occupied. Grazes up to 400 m from the burrow. In cold weather they do not leave their holes.

FOOD: Seeds, stems, leaves, tubers and rhizomes of grass.

VOCALISATION: Normally silent, but scream loudly when handled.

BREEDING: 1, occasionally 2, young are born 2–3 times a year after a gestation period of ± 10 weeks. ♀ has 1 pair of breast mammae.

AGE: ± 7 years.

105

PORCUPINE *Hystrix africaeaustralis*
(YSTERVARK)

SUBSPECIES
None.

Mass: ♂ 10–19 kg
♀ 10–24 kg

Length: ± 84 cm

IDENTIFICATION: Region's largest rodent. The body is covered with charac‑
teristic sharp, black and white quills and flattened bristles.

DIFFERENCE BETWEEN ♂ **AND** ♀: None.

HABITAT: Very adaptable: found in most of the vegetation areas. Prefers broke‑
country with rocky hills and rocky reefs. Shelters in caves, crevices, antbear and othe‑
holes that it adapts. Sometimes a large number of bones can be seen around the hole‑
which have been carried there. Independent of water.

HABITS: Although three or four make use of the same shelter, they often roan‑
alone. Nocturnal, but it lies in the sun at the edge of its shelter. Stands quite still whe‑
disturbed and is often overlooked. Moves noisily down footpaths as it rubs, grunt‑
and sniffs. A noisy grazer. Attacks instinctively sideways or backwards so that th‑
quills remain in the attacker. Seems clumsy but can run quickly.

FOOD: Digs for tubers, bulbs and roots. Fruit, bark, carrion and vegetables.

VOCALISATION: Rattles the tail quills, grunts, sniffs, and chatters the teeth.

BREEDING: 1–3 young are born anytime during the year (summer rainfall areas‑
August–March) after a gestation period of ± 3 months. ♀ has 2 pairs of chest mamma‑
to the sides.

AGE: ± 20 years.

GREATER CANE RAT *Thryonomys swinderianus*
(GROOT RIETROT)

6,5 cm

Mass:	♂	± 4,54 kg
	♀	± 3,58 kg
Length:	♂	± 72 cm
	♀	± 67 cm

IDENTIFICATION: Largest of the two cane rats. Brown with yellow speckles, tiny hair. The elongated snout hangs over the nostrils.

DIFFERS FROM OTHER SPECIES: Lesser cane rat: Smaller and the tail is much shorter than that of the greater cane rat. Utilizes a different habitat.

DIFFERENCE BETWEEN ♂ AND ♀: The male is larger than the female.

HABITAT: Specialized requirements: Reed beds along rivers and dams or tall thick-stemmed grass in the vicinity of vleis, lakes, dams, floodplains or rivers. Dependent on water. Frequent sugar cane plantations.

HABITS: Lives in small groups of 8–10, but grazes alone. Mainly nocturnal, and also active at dawn. Tramples clear footpaths between reed beds and tall grass, where it can move unseen. Rests in thick shelter of reeds or in holes in the river bank or beneath thick vegetation. If chased along the footpath, it runs a distance, stops till the pursuer is close and repeats the action. Swims very well.

FOOD: Roots, stems and sprouts of reeds and grass.

VOCALISATION: Snorts when it grazes. Stamps rear paws and makes a loud whistle as an alarm.

BREEDING: 4–8 young are born from August–December after a gestation period of 4–5 months. ♀ has 3 pairs of breast mammae.

AGE: Unknown.

Dung

The texture and colour of dung can vary depending on what the animal h[as] foraged, and how fresh the droppings are. It can also vary in different [re]gions. In some regions antelope even forage on soil as a salt suppleme[nt.] Predators' dung usually contains more hair, sometimes only hair. The c[ol]our is darker when a lot of blood has been consumed. However, the du[ng] of some predators, such as hyaena, is usually white (see diet).

The texture of the dung varies, especially among smaller predators b[ut] to a lesser extent among antelope. Although the dung of some antelop[e] such as the waterbuck, usually cakes, this also occurs among other antelo[pe] as a variation. During early spring the dung appears to be softer and cak[ed] due to foraging on fresh green grass and leaf sprouts (see example belo[w]).

Other interesting facts about animal dung appear with the photograp[hs.]

This photograph shows the difference between caked and separa[te] droppings of the same animal.

① Red duiker ② Suni ③ Red lechwe ④ Blue wildebeest

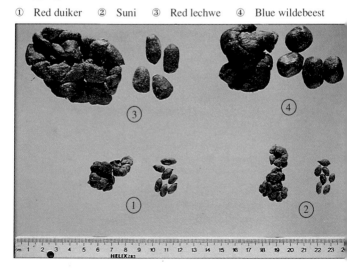

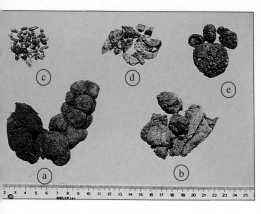

Photo 1:

a) Chacma baboon
b) Samango monkey
c) Lesser bushbaby
d) Thick-tailed bushbaby
e) Vervet monkey

Baboon droppings are found in abundance on cliffs and beneath trees in which they sleep.

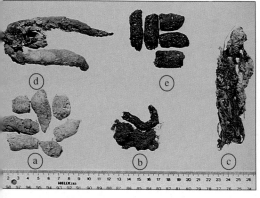

Photo 2:

a) Small spotted cat
b) Polecat
c) Cape fox
d) Small-spotted genet
e) Bat-eared fox

Bat-eared foxes usually defecate close to other dung heaps or sometimes on a common dung heap.

109

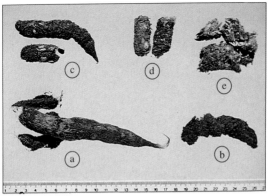

Photo 3:

a) Serval
b) African civ[et]
c) Large-spott[ed] genet
d) Spotted-necked otte[r]
e) Cape clawless ot[ter]

Serval: Defecates without digging or covering the dung – only scratches on[e] with its hind paws. African civet: They defecate on common dung heaps alo[ng] their routes. Both the otters use dung heaps: The Cape clawless otter's du[ng] heaps are usually close to the water – many crab shells are found in them.

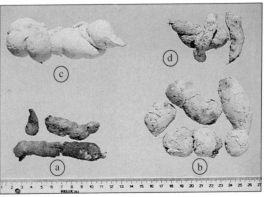

Photo 4:

a) Side-stripe[d] jackal
b) Spotted hyaena
c) Brown hya[ena]
d) Black-back[ed] jackal

Droppings of both hyaenas are green when fresh and white when dry. Both ma[ke] use of common dung heaps usually close to the boundaries of their territorie[s]

110

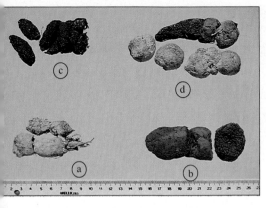

Photo 5:
a) African wild cat
b) Aardwolf
c) Honey badger
d) Caracal

African wild cat: Digs a small hole and covers the droppings with its front paws.
Aardwolf: Defecates on oval dung heaps, first digging a trench and then covering it up.

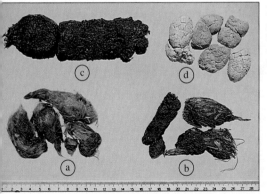

Photo 6:
a) Leopard
b) Cheetah
c) Lion
d) Cape hunting dog

Droppings of leopard are full of hair and may even contain spines of porcupine. Droppings of cheetah are usually darker than those of leopard. Lions' droppings have a distinct scent, are darker in colour — due to the quantity of blood — and may even contain spines of porcupine.

Photo 7:
a) Black rhinoceros
b) White rhinoceros
c) Elephant
d) Hippo-potamus

The black rhinoceros usually defecates on a communal dung heap, which it ofte kicks apart. Dung contains thorns and branches. White rhinoceros: Territoria bulls defecate on dung heaps and often kick them apart. Its dung is dark gree when fresh and becomes darker when dry. Fresh elephant dung is olive greer initially turns darker and then becomes lighter in colour after 6 hours. Hippc potamus usually scatters its dung in or out of the water by a smack of its tail.

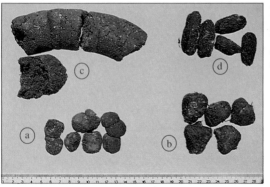

Photo 8:
a) Bushpig
b) Warthog
c) Antbear
d) Porcupine

The antbear's droppings contain a lot of soil and are therefore quite heavy. The usually dig a shallow hole to defecate in and cover it up afterwards.

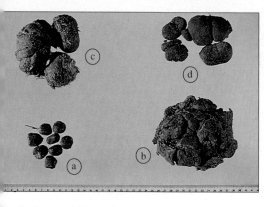

Photo 9:

a) Giraffe
b) Buffalo
c) Mountain zebra
d) Burchell's zebra

Giraffe dung could be confused with that of the kudu, but tends to be scattered more due to the large distance it has to fall. Buffalo dung is similar to that of cattle, but is usually darker in colour. Zebra dung is similar to that of a horse. Mountain zebra droppings are larger than those of Burchell's zebra.

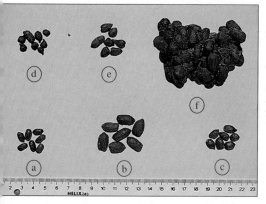

Photo 10:

a) Klipspringer
b) Bontebok/ blesbok
c) Mountain reedbuck
d) Oribi
e) Grey rhebok
f) White-tailed gnu

Klipspringers defecate on common dung heaps within their territories. Bontebok/blesbok: Territorial males defecate on dung heaps in their areas. Oribi males often defecate on dung heaps. White-tailed gnu dung is often caked.

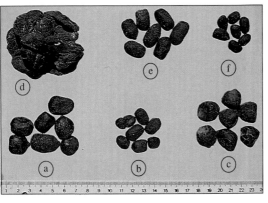

Photo 11:

a) Kudu
b) Nyala
c) Sable antelope
d) Lichtenstein hartebeest
e) Roan antelope
f) Tsessebe

Photo 12:

a) Springbok
b) Gemsbok
c) Eland
d) Blue wildebeest
e) Cape hartebeest
f) Impala

Springbok: Territorial males defecate on conspicuous dung heaps in their territory. Gemsbok: Territorial bulls' droppings form a small heap because they squat when defecating. Blue wildebeest: Droppings are often caked. During the mating season impala rams defecate on conspicuous communal dung heaps (kraals).

114

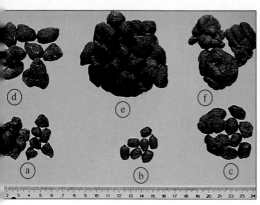

Photo 13:

a) Sitatunga
b) Reedbuck
c) Puku
d) Lechwe
e) Waterbuck
f) Bushbuck

Sitatunga's droppings may be caked. Waterbuck dung is usually caked. Bushbuck's dung is often soft and the droppings fall on top of each other.

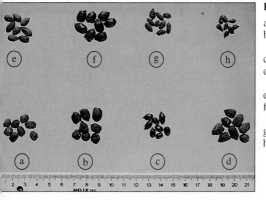

Photo 14:

a) Blue duiker
b) Sharpe's grysbok
c) Steenbok
d) Cape grysbok
e) Red duiker
f) Common duiker
g) Suni
h) Damara dik-dik

Sharpe's grysbok likes to defecate on communal dung heaps. Steenbok defecates on dung heaps mostly on the border of its territory and usually covers the droppings. Damara dik-dik defecates on communal dung heaps, usually combined with a form of ritual.

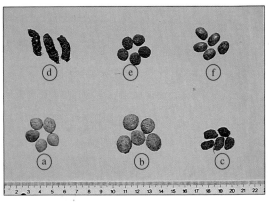

Photo 15:

a) Springhare
b) Scrub hare
c) Dassie
d) Hedgehog
e) Cape hare
f) Greater cane rat

Droppings of rock rabbits are flatter than those of hares and they usually defecate (unlike hares) on common dung heaps some distance from their burrows. Dassies usually defecate on common dung heaps, on klipkoppies or in caves. Greater cane rats defecate along the paths where they forage.

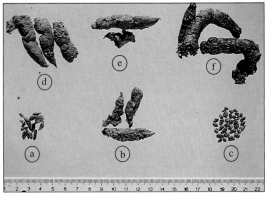

Photo 16:

a) Ground squirrel
b) Yellow mongoose
c) Tree squirrel
d) Banded mongoose
e) Suricate
f) Water mongoose

The dung of the different mongooses look very much alike and it is difficult to distinguish between them.

Spoor and tracking

Tracking is an art that requires a lot of devotion and practice and that should preferably be learned with the assistance of an expert in the field. This book can therefore only be regarded as an aid, but for the beginner there are a few hints to bear in mind. The spoor of specific animals may differ in size and shape, depending on the surface where made. Certain areas of an animal's spoor can be clearly seen in soft or wet soil but not on hard ground. Hooves tend to spread wider in wet or muddy soil to ensure better footing.

Identifying a spoor using this book:

Carefully study the spoor charts as well as the area in which the animal can be found.
Scan the terrain and compare it to the preferred habitat or the habitat keys.
Be on the look-out for other signs close to the animal's spoor (for example droppings) and try to identify the animal; or try to determine what it has foraged on. In this way experts make many interesting observations.

How fresh is the spoor?

To determine this accurately you have to keep in mind the weather conditions of the previous few days: was it windless, or was there rain or wind, and if so, exactly when? For example, when tracking a spoor early in the morning, you may remember that there was some wind about midnight but that the remainder of the night was windless. Then you can determine whether the spoor was made before or after the wind.
Be on the look-out for dung and study it; touch it: if it sticks to your fingers it is quite fresh and if it is still warm, it is obviously very fresh. Use the measurements at the back of the book for measuring the spoor and dung.

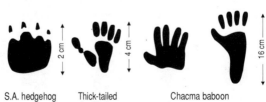

Common mammals

| S.A. hedgehog | Thick-tailed bushbaby | Chacma baboon |

2 cm | 4 cm | 16 cm

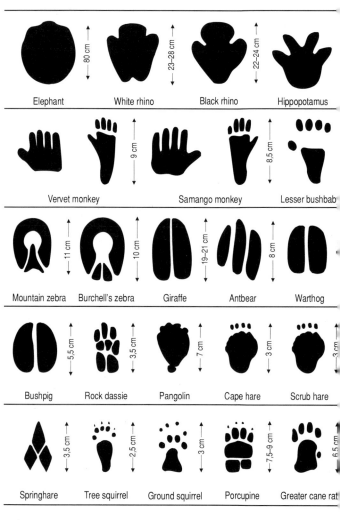

Elephant	White rhino	Black rhino	Hippopotamus

80 cm · 23–28 cm · 22–24 cm

Vervet monkey	Samango monkey		Lesser bushbab

9 cm · 8,5 cm

Mountain zebra	Burchell's zebra	Giraffe	Antbear	Warthog

11 cm · 10 cm · 19–21 cm · 8 cm

Bushpig	Rock dassie	Pangolin	Cape hare	Scrub hare

5,5 cm · 3,5 cm · 7 cm · 3 cm · 3 cm

Springhare	Tree squirrel	Ground squirrel	Porcupine	Greater cane rat

3,5 cm · 2,5 cm · 3 cm · 7,5–9 cm · 6,5 cm

Predators

 4 cm
Bat-eared fox

 8.5 cm
Cape hunting dog

 5 cm
Cape fox

 5 cm
Side-striped jackal

 5,5 cm
Black-backed jackal

 5 cm
Cape clawless otter

 4 cm
Spotted-necked otter

 8,5 cm
Honey badger

 2,5 cm
Striped polecat

 5,5 cm
African civet

 2,5–3 cm
Small-spotted genet

 2,5–3 cm
Large-spotted genet

 3 cm
Suricate

 2,75 cm
Yellow mongoose

 2,5 cm
Slender mongoose

 4 cm
White-tailed mongoose

 4,5 cm
Water mongoose

 3 cm
Banded mongoose

 2,5 cm
Dwarf mongoose

 5,5 cm
Aardwolf

 9–10 cm
Brown hyaena

 9–12 cm
Spotted hyaena

 9–10 cm
Cheetah

 7–12 cm
Leopard

Lion 13 cm   Caracal 5 cm   Serval 4,5 cm   Small spotted cat 2,5 cm   African wild c

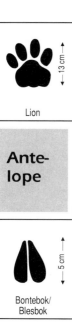

Ante-lope

Black wildebeest 7,5–9,5 cm   Blue wildebeest 9,5–11 cm   Lichtenstein's hartebeest 8–10 cm   Red hartebee

Bontebok/ Blesbok 5 cm   Tsessebe 6–9 cm   Blue duiker 2 cm   Red duiker 2,5 cm   Common duik

Springbok 4,5 cm   Klipspringer 2 cm   Damara dik-dik 2 cm   Oribi 3,5 cm   Steenbok

Cape grysbok 2,5 cm   Sharpe's grysbok 2,5 cm   Suni 2 cm   Impala 5–6 cm   Grey rhebok

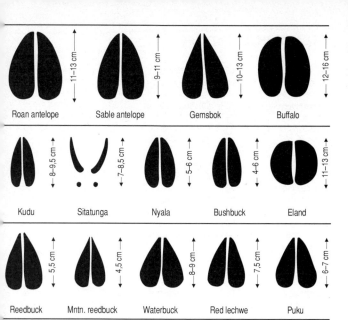

Roan antelope	Sable antelope	Gemsbok	Buffalo
11–13 cm	9–11 cm	10–13 cm	12–16 cm

Kudu	Sitatunga	Nyala	Bushbuck	Eland
8–9,5 cm	7–8,5 cm	5–6 cm	4–6 cm	11–13 cm

Reedbuck	Mntn. reedbuck	Waterbuck	Red lechwe	Puku
5,5 cm	4,5 cm	8–9 cm	7,5 cm	6–7 cm

bibliography

yant, L. 1989. *Rowland Ward's African Records of Big Game (xxii edition)*, San Antonio, Texas: Rowland Ward Publications, a division of Game Conservation International.

lié, B. 1987. *'n Veldgids, Soogdiere van Suider-Afrika.* Sandton: Frandsen Publishers.

 Graaff, G. 1987. *Diere van die Nasionale Krugerwildtuin.* Cape Town: Struik.

rst, J. & Dandelot, P. 1972. *A Field Guide to the Larger Mammals of Africa.* London: Collins.

ester, J.A.J. & Setzer, H.W. 1977. *The Mammals of Africa: An Identification Manual.* Washington D.C.: Smithsonian Institutional Press.

ester, J.A.J. & Rautenbach, I.L. 1986. *Classification of Southern African Mammals.* Pretoria: Transvaal Museum.

naar, U. de V., Joubert, S.C.J., Hall-Martin, A., De Graaff, G. & Rautenbach I.L. 1987. *Veldgids tot die Soogdiere van die Nasionale Krugerwildtuin.* Cape Town: Struik.

naar, U. de V., Rautenbach, I.L., & De Graaff, G. 1980. *The Small Mammals of the Kruger National Park.* Pretoria: National Parks Board of South Africa.

nithers, R.H.N. 1983. *The Mammals of the Southern African Subregion.* Pretoria: University of Pretoria.

alker, C. 1988. *Signs of the wild.* Cape Town: Struik.

Alphabetical index

Photographic acknowledgements

Paul Augustinus: 93(L); Anthony Bannister: 36; Cobie Botha: 67; Willem Botha: 98(L); Koos Delport: 27, 29, 57(R), 100; André du Plessis: 37(L), 51(L); Clem Haagner: 37(R), 39, 47, 101, 105, 106(L); Lex Hes: 22, 23, 38; Peet Joubert: 32; James Maré: 86; Jeanette Matthews, Tvl. Division of Nature and Environmental Conservation: 42, 64; National Parks Board: 35, 52, 54, 62, 65, 81(R), 83 (L+R), 107; Ulrich Oberprieler: 55, 60(L+R); Riaan Wolhuter: 49, 80(L); E.A. Zaloumis, Photographic section of the Wildlife Society of Southern Africa: 33. All other photographs by Burger Cillié.

Burger Cillié uses two Ricoh 35 mm SLR cameras: an XRX and a KR 10M, the latter being sponsored by **Ricoh** of Camcor. He also uses two Tamron lenses: a 70–350 mm f4.5 and a 400 mm f4 LD(IF), the latter being sponsored by **Tamron** of L. Saul.